ELITE • 191

Italian Navy & Air Force Elite Units & Special Forces 1940–45

P. CROCIANI & P.P. BATTISTELLI ILLUSTRATED BY M. STACEY

Series editor Martin Windrow

First published in Great Britain in 2013 by Osprey Publishing,
Midland House, West Way, Botley, Oxford, OX2 0PH, UK
43-01 21st Street, Suite 220B, Long Island City, NY 11101, USA
E-mail: info@ospreypublishing.com

OSPREY PUBLISHING IS PART OF THE OSPREY GROUP

A CIP catalogue record for this book is available from the British Library

Print ISBN: 978 1 84908 857 2
PDF ebook ISBN: 978 1 84908 858 9
ePub ebook ISBN: 978 1 78200 797 5

Editor: Martin Windrow
Index by Fionbar Lyons
Typeset in Sabon and Myriad Pro
Originated by PDQ Media, Bungay, UK

Printed in China through Worldprint Ltd

13 14 15 16 17 10 9 8 7 6 5 4 3 2 1

Osprey Publishing is supporting the Woodland Trust, the UK's leading
woodland conservation charity, by funding the dedication of trees.

www.ospreypublishing.com

ACKNOWLEDGEMENTS

The authors wish to acknowledge the following individuals and institutions
for their help: Archivio Centrale dello Stato, Stefano Ales, Andrea Molinari,
Ufficio Storico Stato Maggiore dell'Esercito, Count Ernesto G. Vitetti, and,
in particular, the Bundesarchiv-Militärarchiv (Freiburg i.Br.), Ufficio Storico
Stato Maggiore Difesa (Rome), Ufficio Storico dello Stato Maggiore della
Marina (Rome), Sottotenente di Vascello Alberto G. Bragadin, the Ufficio
Storico dello Stato Maggiore dell'Aeronautica, Andrea Viotti, Tenente
Colonnello Filippo Cappellano, and the series editor, Martin Windrow.

ABBREVIATED PHOTO CREDITS

AUSSM = Archivio Ufficio Storico Stato Maggiore Marina; Cappellano =
Filippo Cappellano Collection; Crociani = Piero Crociani Collection; Molinari
= Andrea Mollinari Collection; Vitetti = Count Ernesto G. Vitetti Collection

AUTHORS' NOTE

Italian units: In the Italian language male nouns (generally ending in 'o' or
'e') usually take a final 'i' in the plural (e.g., sing. *divisione*, pl. *divisioni;* female
nouns (ending in 'a') take a final 'e' (e.g., sing. *compagnia*, pl. *compagnie*).
Collective titles such as *Arditi* are plural (e.g. sing. *Ardito*). The basic
formations, units and sub-units include an army (*armata*), army corps (*corpo
d'armata*), division (*divisione*), regiment (*reggimento*) and its equivalent
group (*gruppo* or *raggruppamento*), battalion (*battaglione*), company
(*compagnia*), platoon (*plotone*), and squad (*squadra*). Naval units include
flotilla (*flottiglia*) and squadron (*squadriglia*). Ordinal numbers are indicated
by a final superior 'o' when referring to male nouns (e.g. 1° Reggimento),
or 'a' with female nouns (e.g. 2ª Compagnia).

Ranks: For clarity, in this text British equivalents are used for Italian ranks –
see table on page 5.

ARTIST'S NOTE

ABBREVIATIONS & GLOSSARY

ADRA = *Arditi Distruttori Regia Aeronautica*, Air Force assault
engineers

CA, CB = Classes of Caproni midget submarines

FNS = *Forza Navale Speciale*, Special Naval (landing) Force

Gamma = assault frogmen

Mariassalto = Navy assault force on Allied side, 1943–45

MAS = *Motoscafo Armato Silurante*, armed torpedo motorboat

MILMART = *Milizia Artiglieria Marittima*, Fascist coastal artillery militia

MT = *Motoscafo Turismo*, lit. 'leisure motorboat', actually assault boat

MTL = *Motoscafo Trasporto Lento*, slow transport motorboat

MTM = *Motoscafo Turismo Modificato*, improved assault motorboat

MTR = *Motoscafo Turismo Ridotto*, small assault motorboat

MTS = *Motoscafo Turismo Silurante*, torpedo motorboat

MTSM = *MTS Modificato*, improved torpedo motorboat

MTSMA, or SMA = *MTSM Allargato*, improved, widened torpedo
motorboat

SLC = *Siluro Lenta Corsa*, slow manned torpedo

CONTENTS

ITALIAN NAVY & AIR FORCE ELITE UNITS & SPECIAL FORCES 1940–45

INTRODUCTION

It is not easy to give a clear definition of 'elite units' within the context of the Italian Navy and Air Force in World War II. In the broadest sense, operational components of both services were a kind of elite, when compared to a conscript Army with only a minimal number of specialists. However, unlike those of some other nations, the Italian Navy and Air Force never fully developed any kind of 'elite within the elite'; the Italian submarine force never rose to the level of the German *U-Bootswaffe*, while the *Regia Aeronautica*'s torpedo-bomber units – which enjoyed some prestige – never achieved a status comparable with, for instance, the RAF's Pathfinder Force.

It is correct to say of both services that it was their 'special forces' that formed the real elite, regardless of their eventual actual employment. In terms of 'profit and loss', the *10a Flottiglia MAS* undeniably stands out as the real Italian 'elite and special force' during the war: it developed, and used successfully, new weapons and techniques, and achieved a level of specialization and training with few equals amongst either friends or foes.

Compared to this organization, the 'San Marco' naval infantry and the Air Force paratroop and air-landing units inevitably appear as less impressive; nevertheless, all these were developed and trained for a specific mission, which demanded greater and more specialized skills than were required of any others. That mission was the planned assault against the British-held fortress island of Malta, which served as a strategically important air and submarine base in the central Mediterranean.

Essentially, the difference between the successful 10th MAS Flotilla and the less successful Navy and Air Force 'elite' units comes down to the fact that while the former benefited from long preparation, and had opportunities to actually test its weapons and techniques in battle, the latter were neglected or hastily created, and never had a chance to prove themselves in the context that was envisaged. Following the definitive cancellation of the intended assault on Malta, both the 'San Marco' naval infantry and the Air Force airborne troops were employed as conventional infantry, giving them no real opportunity to display their actual skills and capabilities. Italy's surrender on 8 September 1943 not only put an end to

Capitano di Vascello Junio Valerio Borghese, the most famous officer of the Navy special forces. Commander successively of six submarines between 1937 and 1943, and of the Underwater Group of 10th MAS Flotilla, he is pictured here as commander of Xª MAS Flotilla in 1943–45. He wears the grey-green collarless jacket commonly used by all Italian special forces in this period; the white lapel patches, and the white/gold lanyard, are those of the Navy special assault unit after the September 1943 surrender, and the royal crown has been cut from his cap badge. For details of his decorations, see Plate G2. (Vitetti)

any hope of testing them in any kind of special operation, but also radically changed the circumstances and status of the Navy and Air Force specialized units.

The Italian Social Republic, 1943–45

Even before the creation of Mussolini's *Repubblica Sociale Italiana* (RSI) in German-occupied central and northern Italy, the 10th MAS Flotilla and other units – particularly amongst the Army and Air Force paratroopers – rejected the surrender and, in their different ways, showed their determination to continue the fight against the Allies. However, the RSI's armed forces suffered from a contradictory situation: on the one hand, the Germans trusted very few Italian units, and were determined to use all available manpower for their own needs, while on the other, Mussolini and other Fascist leaders were trying to raise Italian armed forces enjoying at least some measure of independence. This led to the creation of a large number of units of very mixed background and quality.

A seaman 1st class of the 'San Marco' Regiment. His service and rating are indicated by the red anchor and single chevron on his sleeves, his appointment as a naval infantry provisional squad leader by the yellow bar on his cuffs, below the Lion of St Mark badges identifying the regiment. He wears the Navy's grey-green dress with field equipment, and carries the Mannlicher Carcano 91TS carbine. Note particularly the Mills-type webbing equipment; apparently inspired by the British 08 set, this differed in having three large, deep cartridge pouches on each side, instead of the five smaller pouches of the British equipment. (AUSSM)

The Germans created many Italian units both for garrison and security duties, and to provide services and supplies to the German combat units; most of these would simply disappear in the summer of 1944, their records being generally unimpressive. The RSI did struggle to create at least the skeleton of an Army (both the Navy and Air Force could only be revived to a limited extent, and mostly under direct German control). By the summer of 1944 the first two RSI divisions were formed and deployed in north-west Italy. Under the circumstances this was a remarkable achievement, but – contrary to the popular image sometimes presented – these were very far from any kind of elite, and despite the large number of units brought into existence in the RSI there were virtually no 'special forces' at all. (The same was true of the monarchy's Italian Liberation Corps formed by the Allies in southern and later central Italy.)

For this reason the new Xᵃ MAS Flotilla, along with the new Air Force 'Folgore' Parachute Regiment, stand out clearly. (The Roman numeral for 'Tenth' was widely used at the time, and in this text it differentiates the post- from the pre-surrender formation.) Both were formed around the cadres of

Equivalent ranks			
Italy *Regia Marina*	**Italy** *Regia Aeronautica*	**Britain** Royal Navy	**Britain** Army
Ammiraglio d'armata	Generale di armata aerea	Admiral	General
Ammiraglio di squadra	Generale di squadra aerea	Vice-Admiral	Lieutenant-General
Ammiraglio di divisione	Generale di divisione aerea	Rear-Admiral	Major-General
Contrammiraglio	Generale di brigata aerea	Commodore 1st Class	–
–	–	Commodore 2nd Class	Brigadier
Capitano di Vascello	Colonnello	Captain	Colonel
Capitano di Fregata	Tenente Colonnello	Commander	Lieutenant-Colonel
Capitano di Corvetta	Maggiore	Lieutenant Commander	Major
Primo Tenente di Vascello	–	–	–
Tenente di Vascello	Capitano	Lieutenant	Captain
Sottotenente di Vascello	Tenente	Sub-Lieutenant	Lieutenant
Guardiamarina	Sottotenente	-	Second Lieutenant
–	–	Midshipman	–

A *secondo capo* (chief petty officer – note yellow chevrons on left breast pocket) of the Xᵃ MAS 'Lupo' Bn, photographed with an *SS-Unterscharführer* (corporal) of 16. SS-PzGren Div 'Reichsführer-SS'. The 'Lupo' Bn was attached to this division for anti-partisan operations in northern Italy from December 1944 to February 1945. The blue lapel patches bear the 'San Marco' lion badge above the wreathed *gladius* of the RSI – see Plate F3. (Cappellano)

elite and special forces that survived the surrender, and both could claim – although to different degrees – better training and skills than most of their counterparts. However, apart from very limited special-forces activities by the Xᵃ MAS Flotilla, both shared a common fate. In a country torn by a civil war in parallel with the fighting between the German and Allied armies, large numbers of partisans confronted the RSI forces and the Wehrmacht alike. Both Xᵃ MAS and 'Folgore', while also fighting the Allied forces, were heavily committed to anti-guerrilla activities, thus once again wasting training and skills that might have been put to better use.

NAVY SPECIAL FORCES: 1ST & 10TH MAS FLOTILLA, 1940–43

Origins

Although the Italian Navy started to test its first motor torpedo boats as early as 1906, it was only after Italy's entry into World War I in May 1915 that development progressed. The first craft was commissioned in April 1915, and was soon in production by the Venetian firm SVAN (*Società Veneziana Automobili Navali*), so was named *Motobarca Armata SVAN*, 'SVAN armed motorboat'. Following mass production by Isotta Fraschini and FIAT as well, it was renamed *Motoscafo Armato Silurante*, 'armed torpedo motorboat', or MAS. (This acronym was also used for *Motoscafo Anti Sommergibile*, 'anti-submarine motorboat', in which role these craft were sometimes used.) The concept of a motor torpedo boat not only introduced a major change to Italian naval doctrine, but also led to development of other special craft. These included the tracked light assault boat, specifically designed to climb over protection nets; and the '*mignatta*' ('leech'), subsequently developed into the *Torpedine Semovente Rossetti* or 'Rossetti self-propelled torpedo' – the first attempt to modify a standard torpedo for manned use.

During World War I the Italian Navy mostly fought against the Austro-Hungarian Navy in the narrow waters of the Adriatic Sea. Both sides tried to avoid any fleet engagement that might have cost them irreplaceable major warships, and this led to the development of craft and tactics for 'small warfare', with the aim of causing as much damage as possible while putting at risk only light and easily replaceable craft. For Italy, this effort was quite successful. By 1918 some 419 MAS had been produced, 244 of them operational; their most significant successes were the sinking of the Austro-Hungarian battleship *Wien* on 9 December 1917, and of the dreadnought *Szent Istvan* on 10 June 1918. But the real step forward was the employment of assault craft, which brought a new dimension to naval warfare. On 13 May 1918 the tracked assault boat *Grillo* ('Cricket') tried to penetrate the Austro-Hungarian naval base of Pola on the Istrian peninsula (today's Pula, Croatia), and though it ultimately failed it did overcome four of the first five obstacles it encountered. Another notable mission – although carried out at the time of the Austro-Hungarian surrender, after the fleet had been handed over to the future Yugoslavia – was the sinking of the battleship *Viribus Unitis* in Pola harbour on 1 November 1918 by a manned torpedo. (This did not really navigate underwater, but was manoeuvred under the bow of the battleship by swimming frogmen.)

* * *

The transformation of the strategic context in the Mediterranean after 1918 brought development of such assault craft to a standstill; the Italian Navy now aimed to become a 'blue-water' service, looking beyond the Adriatic to the whole Mediterranean and, indeed, to the oceans. It was not until 1935–36, when the crisis sparked by Italy's war against Abyssinia (Ethiopia) led to a diplomatic confrontation with Great Britain, that the whole concept of assault craft was revived.[1] In 1935 the Navy engineers Capts Teseo Tesei and Elios Toschi started work on the prototype of a new manned torpedo – basically an evolution of the Rossetti – that was tested in La Spezia harbour in November 1935 and January 1936. Although these tests were unsatisfactory, in April 1936 the Navy asked for four others to be built, and new trials followed that May. The conclusion of the Italian-Abyssinian war that same month brought the manned torpedo project to a standstill, but not the testing of surface assault craft.

In 1935 the Air Force officer Amedeo di Savoia d'Aosta, a member of the royal family, and his brother Aimone, a naval officer, developed the concept of the *motoscafo d'assalto*, 'assault motorboat': a small launch loaded with explosives that could be lifted by air close to enemy ships, set on course to ram them, and abandoned by the pilot just before impact. The first two prototypes were tested in November 1936, by which time the embryo of a future naval light assault force had already been formed. On 15 September 1935 the 1st Submarine Flotilla officially incorporated a cadre of personnel at the La Spezia base to study, develop and train for the use of special craft. Training also started at the bases of Porto Santo Stefano and Bocca di Serchio, and although it was halted in summer 1936, with personnel being sent back to their units and the cadre disbanded, studies and development were not abandoned.

1 See Men-at-Arms 309, *The Italian Invasion of Abyssinia 1935–36*

In the mid-1930s tests were carried out by underwater 'walkers', who were intended to make their way to target ships by walking on the seabed carrying a 50kg explosive charge. For this purpose they were equipped with weighted boots, and a magnetic compass. Trials revealed that visibility was too poor and progress too slow, and the project was abandoned in favour of conventional swimming 'frogmen'. (AUSSM)

1935–36: the second prototype of the *torpedine semovente* (self-propelled torpedo), which differed only in minor details from the original 533mm projectile. Note how the crewmen had to crouch down behind the low, openwork control shields. (AUSSM)

In June 1937 the Naval Staff (*Stato Maggiore Marina*) finally took the project seriously, and eventually, on 28 September 1938, it ordered the creation, within the *1a Flottiglia MAS* (1st Torpedo Motorboat Flotilla) at La Spezia, of a research-and-development detachment (officially named in 1939 *Sezione Armi Speciali*, 'Special Weapons Section'). The detachment had only 21 officers (including Capts Tesei and Toschi) at La Spezia, plus seven others at a secret base at Bocca di Serchio, and six more manning the assault motorboats. Only seven of these craft were available, along with 11 manned torpedoes. On 6 July 1939 the Naval Staff sanctioned the tasks of the 1st MAS Flotilla; despite a report by its commander complaining of the lack of personnel and craft, he was encouraged by the level of training achieved.

On 24 February 1940, less than four months before Italy's entry into World War II on 10 June, command of the 1st MAS Flotilla and of the Special Weapons Section was taken over by Cdr Mario Giorgini. On 10 August 1940 the Naval Staff issued the first operational order, which led to the first (aborted) mission against Alexandria harbour. Two other missions in September against Alexandria and Gibraltar, and one in October against Gibraltar, were all unsuccessful, and during the last of these Cdr Giorgini was captured.

The new flotilla

On 23 January 1941 Cdr Vittorio Moccagatta, who had been developing assault craft in the Aegean, was given command of the Special Weapons Section; and on 15 March this formed the new 10th MAS Flotilla (in fact, a bogus cover title), as part of a major reorganization of the naval assault force. The flotilla was organized with an HQ, including a plans office and a studies section, with the new weapons section under direct control; it had two units (*reparti*), the first controlling the surface assault boats and the training school, under command of LtCdr Giorgio Giobbe, and the second controlling the manned torpedoes under command of LtCdr Junio Valerio

Borghese, who also commanded the submarine *Sciré*. The flotilla also included a training centre for frogmen under command of Lt Angelo Belloni, who had personally invented much of their equipment. Following the death of Cdr Moccagatta on 26 July 1941, Cdr Ernesto Forza took over command of the flotilla until he was replaced by Borghese on 1 May 1943. (Lieutenant-Commander Giobbe would also fall, to be replaced by LtCdr Todaro, who would be killed in his turn.) After further reorganization, in September 1941 the structure of the 10th MAS Flotilla was as follows:

Headquarters (La Spezia): Cdr Ernesto Forza
    Ufficio Operazioni e Addestramento (Ops & Training)
    Comandante al dettaglio (Logistics)
    Servizio Genio Navale (Naval Engineering)
    Servizio Sanitario (Medical)
Naviglio Subacqueo (Underwater Craft): LtCdr Borghese
    Bases at Bocca di Serchio & La Spezia: LtCdr Ernesto Notari
    Operazioni e Addestramento (Ops & Training): LtCdr Borghese
    Scuola Sommozzatori (Frogman School, Livorno): Lt Wolk
    Unità Operanti (operational units): Lt Mario Arillo (incl. surface transport vessels, & carrier submarines *Sciré* and *Ambra*, commanded by Borghese and Arillo)
    Studi e Materiali (Research & Materials): Lt Angelo Belloni
    Gruppo Operativo 'Gamma' (operational group, frogmen)
    Gruppo Operativo SLC (operational group, manned torpedoes)
Naviglio di Superficie (Surface Craft): LtCdr Salvatore Todaro
    Squadriglia MTM, MTSM, MTL (assault & transport motorboat squadron)
    Servizio Tecnico (Technical Services)

The flotilla's main base was at La Spezia on the Tyrrhenian Sea, until moved to nearby Muggiano on 3 September 1942. Surface craft, mostly the ramming motorboats, used La Spezia harbour for training, while the base at Bocca di Serchio, at the mouth of the Serchio river in Tuscany, was used by the manned torpedo crews. The frogman school was established at the Naval Academy at Livorno on 1 September 1940 under command of Lt Wolk, with the expert technical support of Lt Belloni. This trained both the crews of the manned torpedoes and the Gamma swimming saboteurs; the 'N' unit of the 'San Marco' Naval Inf Regt also trained here until early 1942, when they moved to Tarquinia to train alongside the 'P' unit parachutists (see below).

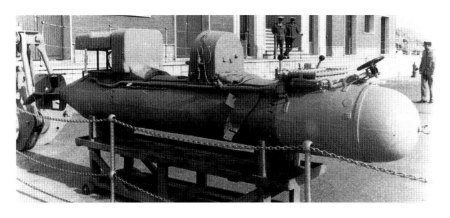

The Series 100 '*maiale*' used by Capt Teseo Tesei during the failed attack on shipping in Gibraltar harbour on 28/29 October 1940. The auto-destruct device failed, and the 'hog' was recovered on the beach at La Linea – minus the warhead, here replaced – by the neutral but friendly Spanish authorities. (AUSSM)

An advanced base would be established in Sicily in 1941, and several improvised bases would be used during the war. These included – most dramatically – the Italian tankers *Fulgor* and *Olterra* that were interned (conveniently) in the neutral Spanish harbours of Cadiz and Algeciras. These were used clandestinely by frogmen and manned torpedo crews for attacks against Gibraltar, the *Olterra* being modified to allow underwater access.

It is noteworthy that until 6 February 1942 the assault forces (both as part of the 1st and later the 10th Flotilla) were under the direct command of the Naval Staff. On that date a General Inspectorate of MAS (abbreviated as *Generalmas*) was formed at Livorno under the now Vice-Adm Aimone di Savoia Aosta, with responsibility for both the 10th MAS Flotilla and the 'San Marco' Regiment. This was in fact a cover name for the naval special forces command, which only in April 1943 took responsibility for inspection duties over the actual MAS units. The HQ was moved to Lerici, near La Spezia, in spring 1942.

CRAFT AND EQUIPMENT

The Italian Navy was a pioneer in the development of types of craft that would later be produced for other navies: the Royal Navy's 'Chariot' manned torpedoes; the German Kriegsmarine's *Linsen* piloted assault motorboats, and *Neger* and *Marder* manned torpedoes; and the Imperial Japanese Navy's *Shynyo* suicide boats and *Kaiten* manned suicide torpedoes.[2]

2 See Elite 177, *German Special Forces of World War II*, and New Vanguard 180, *Kamikaze: Japanese Special Attack Weapons 1944–45*

An improved SLC (*siluro lenta corsa*, 'slow speed torpedo') Series 200; produced from 1941, this type was used for the first time at Alexandria in December 1941. (AUSSM)

10TH MAS FLOTILLA; ITALY, 1941–42
(1) Manned torpedo crewman, 1941
(2) Frogman, Gamma group, 1942
The two-man crews of the '*maiali*' (background) and the assault swimmers both wore the waterproof suit invented by Angelo Belloni. This had an internal rubber layer, and an external suit of rubberized canvas; the different sections were sewn together, and the seams reinforced with glued strips – stronger for manned-torpedo crews than for free swimmers. Frogmen used rubber swim-fins (two models illustrated), but these were too cumbersome for the 'hog' crews. On operations, both could wear over their heads and shoulders a camouflage net made to resemble seaweed (not illustrated here), and applied black cream to their faces and hands. The re-breather apparatus, originally invented by Pirelli in 1935–36 and developed during the war, featured two high-pressure cylinders of pure oxygen. This was diluted with exhaled air in the chest-mounted 'lung' before being channeled through a valve to the mouthpiece; exhaled air passed into a soda-lime container that 'scrubbed' it of carbon dioxide so that it could be inhaled again. This design prevented tell-tale bubbles rising to the surface. Large, high-quality wrist watches and wrist compasses were issued.

(3) *Tenente di vascello*, service dress, 1940
This officer, of the senior of the two grades of lieutenant, wears standard Navy blue service dress with peaked cap; the 10th MAS wore no special insignia. The line officer's cap badge is a fouled anchor on a blue cushion between gold leaves surmounted by a gold crown; the cap band and the cuffs of the 'reefer' jacket show the three narrow gold stripes of this rank, the upper cuff stripe with a round 'curl'. The national silver star of Savoy is worn on the lapels, and gold transverse tabs on the shoulders. The ribbons indicate the War Merit Cross, War Service Badge, and silver Sports Medal.

1

2

3

Manned torpedoes

The first of the manned torpedoes was the *Siluro Lenta Corsa* (SLC), 'slow speed torpedo', nicknamed the *maiale* or 'hog', first developed by Tesei and Toschi in 1935–36. By summer 1939 about 11 of these were available, but it was not until July 1940 that the new generation entered production. These were designated Series 100, and followed in 1941 by the improved Series 200. They were based on the standard 533mm torpedo with suitable adaptations: the double propellers were replaced by a single larger one in an enclosed structure to prevent snagging on nets, and seats for two crewmen and superstructures housing controls were added. The SLC weighed from 1.3 to 1.4 tons, and measured between 6.7 and 7.3m (22–24ft). The 1.6hp electric motor gave a speed of 2–3 knots, to a depth of between 15m and a theoretical maximum of 30m (49–98ft). Once they reached their target the two crewmen had to detach the 1.8m (5.9ft) explosive warhead; this contained a charge of between 230kg and 260kg (507lb–573lb), or, in the last model, two 125kg (275lb) charges. By September 1943 some 50 examples had been built; by then they were largely outdated in comparison with the British 'Chariots' and the new Italian *Siluro San Bartolomeo* (SSB) – though only three prototypes of this greatly improved model had been built by the time of the Italian surrender.

Gamma assault swimmers

Both the 'hog' crewmen and the Gamma assault swimmers used Belloni rubberized suits and closed-circuit re-breathing apparatus. The frogman school, which developed assault tactics from September 1940, was very selective; it was hard to pass the ten-month course, and only some 50 Gamma assault swimmers saw action during the war. Their task was to carry to the targets explosive charges (called *cimici*, 'bugs', and *bauletti*, 'little trunks'), weighing respectively 4.5kg and 12kg (9.9lb & 26lb); a skilled frogman could carry either five *cimici* or two *bauletti*. Both these charges, like the *maiali* warheads, could be fastened to the hull of a ship and detonated using a timer device.

'*Maiali*' crewmen during training, wearing the Belloni suit and the re-breather apparatus also employed by the Gamma assault frogmen; see Plate A1. On shore the suit had to be worn with sandals, to prevent tearing of the rubber feet. This ARO Model 49 breathing apparatus has two separate eyepieces; the improved Model 50 had a single-piece mask. The apparatus had a maximum endurance of six hours. (Vitetti)

Transport to the target area

The key issue for both the 'hogs' and the Gamma swimmers was the approach to the target area. The limited range provided by the endurance of the breathing apparatus (maximum six hours) and of the 'hog' (no more than 4 miles/6.5km at operational speed, though up to 15 miles/24km at cruising speed) made the use of transport vessels necessary. These were either surface or underwater carriers; the former were also used to take the limited-range ramming motorboats close to their targets.

The surface transports ranged from destroyers adapted as carriers (the *Quintino Sella* and *Francesco Crispi*, which took part in the 25/26 March 1941 attack in Suda Bay, Crete), and the escort *Diana* (used for the 25/26 July 1941 attack against Malta), to other motorboats. Some were used for towing the assault boats, in particular MAS 451, 452, 509, 556 & 562, used in the attacks against Malta in the summer of 1941. For this task the *Motosiluranti* (larger, conventional motor torpedo boats) MS 74 & 75 were also made available from late June 1943. Additionally, civilian freighters and fishing boats were used, mostly by 10th MAS Flotilla units in North Africa.

The innovative *Motoscafo Trasporto Lento*, 'slow transport motorboat', was a wooden craft 8.5m long by 2.9m wide (28ft × 9.5ft) specifically developed to carry manned torpedoes on the last leg of their journey before the attack, but it had a limited range of 60 miles (96.5km) at 5 knots cruising speed. Their limited availability made their operational use infrequent, and the one employed during the June 1941 attack against Malta was eventually scuttled.

It did not take long to realize that a better way to carry manned torpedoes close to their targets was underwater, and that – much to the contrary of initial assessments – adapted Class 600 'Mediterranean' submarines were ideal for the purpose. In the first months of 1940 the Class 600 *Ametista*, under command of LtCdr Borghese, started trials as a 'hog' carrier at La Spezia; the *maiali* were mounted on racks on the deck, which (amongst other problems) restricted the maximum dive depth to 30m (98ft). The Class 600 *Iride* was converted in July 1940, and saw limited use before it was sunk on 21 August. Its replacement, the Class 600 *Gondar*, was no luckier; it was converted as a carrier in August 1940, only to be sunk during the aborted

A Series 200 'hog' is lifted aboard a surface transport craft at Bocca di Serchio in 1941. Immediately behind the pilot's seat is the crash-dive tank; the structure behind the second crewman's position is a simple counterbalance for the weight of the engine. (AUSSM)

The submarine *Gondar* at La Spezia in early September 1940, with the three cylindrical chambers used to carry manned torpedoes clearly visible (two on the forrard deck, one aft). Sighted while approaching Alexandria on 29 September, the boat was sunk after a 14-hour chase. (AUSSM)

mission of 30 September. Nevertheless, it had brought one definitive improvement: its deck was fitted with three cylindrical metal containers that could be flooded from inside the submarine, thereby enabling it to reach the standard 90m (295ft) safety depth.

In August–September 1940 the Class 600 submarine *Sciré* was adapted as a carrier, this time with four containers. At first commanded by Borghese and later by LtCdr Bruno Zelich, it eventually became the most successful underwater carrier used by the 10th MAS, until it was sunk on 10 August 1942. It took part in the failed missions against Gibraltar of January and October 1940 and May 1941, and the successful missions against Gibraltar in September 1941 and Alexandria in December 1941. It was replaced by the Class 600 *Ambra*; converted in October 1941 and first used for the May 1942 mission against Alexandria, it was eventually sunk on 9 September 1943.

Photo from a sequence showing how an SLC crew operated from a carrier submarine. At periscope depth, the crewmen emerged from the deck escape hatch; they opened the flooded deck container, extracted the 'hog', and then rode it towards the target, initially cruising just below the surface. It was hoped that they could return to the submarine after attaching their warhead to the hull of an enemy vessel. (AUSSM)

The only ocean-going submarine converted for carrier use was the *Leonardo da Vinci*, adapted to carry a midget submarine for a planned attack against the United States. Three other submarines – *Murena*, *Sparide* and *Grongo* – were adapted between February and May 1943 to carry reduced-height assault motorboats (see below); they were never used by the 10th MAS, and were pressed into German service after the Italian surrender. The Class 600 *Aradam* was still being converted in September 1943; the Germans put it at the disposal of the Xª MAS, but it was never used on operations of any kind.

Assault motorboats

The first boats tested in November 1936 weighed one ton and had a length of 4.7m (15.4ft). It was intended that the boat's top speed of 32.4 knots would enable it to get close to enemy vessels, avoiding their fire by speed and manoeuvrability, until it could be aimed directly towards the selected target. At the very last moment the pilot would fix the wheel and abandon the boat, which would explode either on contact or, by means of a delay fuse, after the crashed boat and its explosive charges had sunk to a certain depth. (While surviving an attack demanded great courage, judgement and good luck, it must be emphasized that the Italian ramming boats were never intended as *kamikaze*-style suicide weapons.)

The production of the first series of '*barchini*' – 'little boats', the nickname for all such craft – started only in late 1938, with the first six examples delivered in spring 1939. These were of the *Motoscafo Turismo* (MT) type, translating roughly as 'leisure motorboat' – a designation that seems highly ironic, given their mission. The subsequent *MT Modificato* (MTM), first tested in November 1940, was 6.1m (20ft) long. Both types could carry a 300–330kg (660–727lb) explosive charge in the bow, at a top speed of 31 knots; the MTM had the important improvement of a special seatback-cum-liferaft fitted behind the pilot that he used during the 'jump' and while awaiting rescue. Only a dozen MTs were produced, but some 40 MTMs. Early in 1941 a reduced-size *MT Ridotto* was produced; with a height of only 1.14m (3.7ft), they could be carried inside the deck cylinders of carrier submarines without reducing the size of the explosive charge, but in fact they were never used in this way.

Another innovation was the *MT Siluranti* (MTS), 'torpedo motorboat', a launch armed with one or two small torpedoes, that would have greater manoeuvrability than conventional motor torpedo boats. Available early in 1941, the first examples could reach a top speed of 28 knots with a maximum range of 158km (98 miles), and were armed with two modified 450mm torpedoes. An improved *MTS Modificato* (MTSM) entered service in spring 1942; this had a top speed of 32–34 knots and a range of 320km (200 miles), although armed with only one torpedo and two 50kg (110lb) bombs. At the time of the Italian surrender just three examples of a new 'improved and widened' *MTSM Allargato* (MTSMA or SMA) were available; these had a top speed of 29–30 knots and a range of 400km (250 miles) carrying a single torpedo.

Early MTM ramming motorboats during training in 1940–41. These craft had an overall length of about 20ft, a beam of 5ft 6in, and a height of less than 4ft; they could manoeuvre at about 30 knots, making them a small and elusive target, especially after dark. Note the rail around the bow of the further boat, just below the gunwale; when the boat struck, this '*palmola*' activated a small charge that sank it, and the main charge of around 700lb of high explosive would be detonated by a hydrostatic trigger when it reached a more damaging depth below the target ship's waterline. (AUSSM)

The MAS boat itself (*Motoscafo Armato Silurante*, 'armed torpedo motorboat') saw only limited use by the flotilla, in 1942–45. Up to June 1940, 50 of the Class 500 MAS were built, with another 25 over the following year, in four versions. The Class 500 was 18.7m long by 4.7m in the beam (61.3 × 15.4ft), displacing 22–29.4 tons. It had a crew of 9 to 13, and was armed with two 450mm torpedoes, 6–10 depth charges, and one 13.2mm heavy MG, replaced in 1941 with a Breda 20mm cannon. It had a top speed of up to 44 knots, and a range of between 645km and 1,600km (400–1,000 sea miles).

OPERATIONS

1940
As in many other cases, pre-war lethargy and indecision at the highest levels of the Italian military greatly hampered the combat units when war came. Early naval special operations suffered from limited availability of craft and other equipment, from still-incomplete testing and training, from the Navy Staff's slow reaction to the changing situation in the Mediterranean, and from its early reluctance to use these new weapons. Only on 10 August 1940 was the first operational order issued to the assault section of the 1st MAS Flotilla; operation 'GA 1' was to be an attack against the British Royal Navy's main harbour at Alexandria, Egypt – more than 1,500 miles from the flotilla's La Spezia base. On 12 August the submarine *Iride* left La Spezia carrying four SLC manned torpedoes, but on 21 August it was sighted and sunk in the Gulf of Bomba by three RAF torpedo-bombers. The second mission against Alexandria on 21 September, 'GA 2' by the submarine *Gondar* carrying three SLC, was also sighted and attacked by RAF aircraft on 29–30 September; the boat eventually sank, and among its captured crew was Capt Mario Giorgini, commanding officer of the 1st MAS Flotilla.

Borghese's submarine *Sciré* left La Spezia on 24 September 1940 carrying three SLC on mission 'BG 1', intending to attack major Royal Navy assets in Gibraltar harbour (some 800 miles away), but the mission was aborted on the 29th on receipt of news that the British 'Force H' had already sailed from the Rock. On 21 October the *Sciré* left La Spezia for Gibraltar once again, carrying three SLC for mission 'BG 2'. This time the objective was reached, and at 2.19am on the 29th the SLC were released, eventually making it into the harbour. One broke down just before reaching the battleship HMS *Barham*, and the other two (piloted by Capt Tesei and SubLt de la Penne) had to abort due to the failure of their breathing apparatus. The crewmen managed to reach the Spanish coast to be rescued and brought back to Italy, and one of the 'hogs' was eventually recovered by the Spanish authorities.

1941
In March 1941 the assault motorboats of the new 10th MAS Flotilla had their baptism of fire at Suda Bay during the fierce battles for the island of Crete. Carried in by the destroyers *Francesco Crispi* and *Quintino Sella*, at 2.45am on 26 March six MT (two others had been damaged in an air attack) were launched to attack British ships at anchor, hitting and damaging the heavy cruiser HMS *York* and the tanker *Pericles*. The *York* was only prevented from sinking by running aground, where it became easy prey for air attacks and was eventually abandoned; the *Pericles* sank while being towed back to Alexandria. All the 'barchini' crews survived to be taken

prisoner. The 10th MAS's first success was followed by another failure: an armed reconnaissance carried out by two MTS towed by two MAS to the island of Corfu on 4/5 April was aborted after being spotted by land defences.

Borghese and the *Sciré* were back in action on the night of 26/27 May at Gibraltar; after their crews were taken aboard from the tanker *Fulgor* in Cadiz harbour three SLC were released, but the mission failed. No targets were attacked and all the 'hogs' were lost, though the rescued crews were eventually brought back to Italy.

An advanced base was created at Augusta, Sicily, in time for the attacks against Valletta, Malta, on 24 and 30 June. Towed by MAS, eight MT tried to attack the Grand Harbour on both nights without success, losing two MT and never entering the anchorage; another attack on the 28th was aborted.

The 'jump' from a MTM assault motorboat, photographed at the Xᵃ MAS training school at Sesto Calende in spring 1944. The launch travels at full speed; after aiming it at the target vessel the pilot locks the rudder, and throws himself backwards into the water, complete with the back of his seat. In the third photo a pilot has unfolded this into a small liferaft, on which he awaits rescue – in practice, he could usually only hope to be picked up by the enemy. This pilot wears a Belloni protective suit. (AUSSM)

This failure foreshadowed the outcome of a dramatic combined attack by 'hogs' and motorboats against Valletta on 26/27 July. The attackers were spotted; they succeeded in destroying St Elmo's Bridge, while penetrating the harbour, but they never got out again. Eight out of nine MT were destroyed and the ninth was captured intact by the British, while two 'hogs', two MAS and one MTL were lost. Only the MTS made it back, with 11 survivors out of the 50 crewmen; among the casualties was Cdr Moccagatta, commander of 10th MAS Flotilla.

Despite this dispiriting string of failures, the flotilla's subsequent reorganization was finally crowned with success. On 10 September 1941 the *Sciré* sailed from La Spezia carrying three SLC and, after collecting the crews from the *Fulgor* in Cadiz, at 1.07am on the 20th it released them at the entrance to Gibraltar harbour. This mission 'BG 4' sank the tanker *Fiona Shell* and inflicted damage on the tanker *Denbydale* and the freighter *Durham*, all the *maiali* crewmen making their way back to Italy successfully.

This was the curtain-raiser for 10th MAS's greatest achievement. On 3 December 1941 the *Sciré*, commanded by Borghese, left La Spezia again for mission 'GA 3' against far-off Alexandria. On the night of 18/19 December the three SLC were released; they damaged the battleships HMS *Valiant* and *Queen Elizabeth* seriously enough to put them out of action for more than a year, along with the tanker *Sagona*, at the cost of the six crewmen captured. This Italian success left the Royal Navy with only three light cruisers and a handful of destroyers in the east and central Mediterranean, altering the balance of naval forces in favour of the Axis. One can only imagine what the consequences might have been had an assault been mounted against Malta early in 1942.

1942–43

A subsequent attempt to finish off HMS *Queen Elizabeth* on 12 May 1942 (operation 'GA 4') ended in failure due to the increased countermeasures and defences, which suggested a switch to the employment of the Gamma frogmen to place charges against Allied vessels.

The first Gamma mission was carried out by 12 frogmen from the converted tanker *Olterra* in Algeçiras harbour against Gibraltar. This operation 'GG 1' took place on the night of 13/14 July 1942; the swimmers

B **10TH MAS FLOTILLA & MIDGET SUBMARINES, 1940–42**

(1) *Sottotenente di vascello*, 'barchino' pilot; Italy, 1942
Before the Belloni suit was adopted by the assault-boat pilots they used either Navy uniform or a working overall, here with canvas shoes for ease of swimming. The improved 1942 life vest, with a collar designed to keep the head out of the water, was of orange canvas stuffed with kapok; the small buttoned pocket on the right and the larger one on the left accommodated a medical kit and water bottle. This sub-lieutenant wears the white summer cap, with the two band stripes of his rank.

(2) *Marinaio*, fatigue dress; Italy, 1940
This seaman wears one of the Navy's several working uniforms of a grey woollen blouse complete with plain sailor's collar, bearing no trim or badges of rank, and wide, straight trousers worn over black leather shoes. Depending on climate this was worn over a white T-shirt or a grey or dark blue wool jumper. This grey version of the sailor's hat might be replaced with a grey beret. Sometimes cloth unit insignia might be sewn to the left chest, such as the naval infantry's Lion of St Mark (see Plate C1a); here, **detail 2a** shows the metal pin-on model of the submariner's dolphin badge. This seaman carries an old-pattern life vest.

(3) *Tenente di vascello*, 1st 'CB' Submarine Squadron; Yalta, Crimea, summer 1942
Midget-submarine crews shared the generally relaxed naval attitude to shipboard dress. This boat commander wears a privately purchased zip-up jacket with an open shirt, fatigue trousers and heavy leather shoes. Unlike their German counterparts, Italian submarine commanders did not identify their appointment by wearing white summer caps all year round, but wore white or blue according to season.

Tenente di Vascello Luigi Durand de la Penne, the SLC pilot who on 19 December 1941 severely damaged the battleship HMS *Queen Elizabeth*, flagship of Adm Sir Andrew Cunningham, C-in-C British Mediterranean Fleet, in Alexandria harbour. Captured before the charge exploded, he would be awarded the Gold Medal for Military Valour in 1944, after the Italian surrender. It is pleasant to record that Cunningham – by then Admiral of the Fleet and First Sea Lord – attended the ceremony. (AUSSM)

succeeded in damaging four cargo ships, and further success was only prevented by faulty charges. Operation 'SL 1', a planned attack against Haifa harbour by eight swimmers, started on 27 July but ended on 10 August when the submarine *Sciré* was sunk off the coast of Palestine. Another mission against Gibraltar ('GG 2') by three swimmers from the *Olterra* took place on 14 September, sinking the cargo ship *Ravens Point*. Gamma attacks against Malta's submarine base were planned in November 1942 ('GG 1–2'), but were aborted because of the weather, as was a mission in April 1943. Other missions against Allied-held Bône harbour in Algeria on 12/14 December 1942 and 5/6 April 1943 would also be aborted; at the end of the first, an Allied air raid led to the death of Cdr Todaro.

Between August and September 1942 the '*autocolonna Giobbe*' – a motorized column carrying MTM and MTSM boats – operated along the coast of North Africa; its main success was damaging the destroyer HMS *Eridge* on 29 August. For months to come missions were still carried out either against Gibraltar from the *Olterra* or against less heavily defended harbours. On 7 December 1942 three SLC from the *Olterra* attacked Gibraltar without success ('BG 5'); however, mission 'BG 6' carried out on 8 May 1943 by three more 'hogs' ended with three cargo ships damaged and the three SLC returning safely to base. The last attack against Gibraltar took place on 3/4 August 1943 ('BG 7'); three cargo ships were sunk, and the three SLC, minus one crewman, made their way back to the *Olterra*.

The tide of war in the Mediterranean was turning decisively against the Axis, and the activities of the Italian Navy special assault craft entered their last phase. On 10 December 1942 the submarine *Ambra* carried three SLC (for the first time with new 150kg warheads) and ten frogmen to attack Algiers harbour (operation 'NA 1'); they were all taken prisoner, but sank one cargo ship and damaged two others. The last two missions were Operation *Stella*, from and against ships in neutral Turkish harbours, where between 30 June and 30 July 1943 a single Gamma frogman sank three British cargo vessels; and, on 18 July, an attempt against Allied ships in Syracuse harbour, Sicily, using three MTR from the carrier submarine *Ambra*. The latter was attacked and damaged before the mission could be launched, eventually making its way back to base. Less than two months later Italy's surrender started a wholly new phase in the history of the 10th MAS Flotilla.

* * *

A summary of operations shows that between 10 June 1940 and 8 September 1943 the *Regia Marina* special assault craft sank three warships and nine cargo ships, for a total of more than 60,000 gross tonnage. These few sailors with their light craft thus accounted for 12 per cent of the Italian Navy's total sinkings in the Mediterranean (including mines), and more than 25 per cent in terms of tonnage. Including the ships they damaged, the figures are 38 per cent of the warships and 15 per cent of the cargo vessels. This was at the cost of 20 Italians killed and 53 taken prisoner, out of a total of just 238 men employed in these operations.

MIDGET SUBMARINES
& THE BLACK SEA

The Italian Navy took delivery of its first midget submarines in absolute secrecy in April 1938; called CA-1 and CA-2 (after the manufacturer, Caproni), these were coastal-defence boats based on World War I experience. The CA boats had a displacement of 13 tons and a two-man crew, and carried two 450mm torpedoes; only 10m (32.8ft) long, they could easily be transported by rail or road. Lack of underwater manoeuvrability and teething problems led to the development by Caproni in 1940 of the type B midget submarine, the first two (CB-1 and CB-2) being delivered at La Spezia on 27 January 1941, and four others (CB-4 to -6) on 10 May. With the same armament, this new boat was more than just an evolution of the CA; it displaced 36 tons surfaced (45 tons submerged), with a maximum surface speed of 7.5 knots (7 knots submerged), and had greatly improved seagoing and manoeuvre capabilities. It had a four-man crew, while still retaining a limited size of 15m long by 3m wide (49.2 × 9.8ft). The CB proved fully satisfactory at the first trials, and although at that time no real need for them had been formulated, the 1st CB Submarine Squadron was formed by mid-1941 with the six available boats. They were deployed to the southern Tyrrhenian Sea (Naples–Salerno) to serve – fruitlessly – as submarine hunters.

In April 1942 the German and Italian navies held a joint conference during which the former specifically asked for Italian naval support on the Eastern Front. This led to the deployment to the Black Sea of a mixed Italian naval force; the units left Italy on 25 April 1942 by road to Vienna, whence the vessels continued their journey to the Black Sea down the Danube. On 2 May they reached Constanza on the Romanian coast, crossing from there to their operational base at Yalta in the Crimea. The units were under command of 4th MAS Flotilla (Cdr Francesco Mimbelli), and included:

Summer 1942: at the base established by 10th MAS Flotilla at Foros on the Black Sea, LtCdr Salvatore Todaro watches sailors checking a 450mm torpedo ready for loading aboard one of the MTSM torpedo motorboats of the 'colonna Moccagatta'. (AUSSM)

1ᵃ Squadriglia Sommergibili 'CB' (Lt Lesen Aston d'Aston, later Lt Giovanni Sorrentino, & Cdr Alberto Torri), with the six CB boats

XIX Squadriglia MAS (LtCdr Castagnacci, later Lt de Giorgi), with four MAS torpedo motorboats

XVII Squadriglia MAS (Lt Ciccoli, later Lt Freschi), as *XIX Squadriglia*

101ᵃ Squadriglia MAS – the motorized '*colonna Moccagatta*', named after the 10th MAS Flotilla's fallen commander (LtCdr Aldo Lenzi, later LtCdr Salvatore Todaro), with five MTSM and five smaller boats.

Neither the midget submarines nor the 10th Flotilla's motorboats had an easy time. Because of their limited speed and range the CBs were deployed close offshore for missions lasting only two nights and one day, mainly trying to intercept Soviet submarines that were carrying supplies into the encircled fortress of Sebastopol or evacuating wounded and high-ranking officers. On 13 June 1942 CB-5 was sunk off Yalta by a Soviet torpedo boat; but two days later CB-3 attacked and sank the Soviet submarine S-32, and on 18 June CB-2 also attacked and claimed another (SC-213 according to Soviet sources, SC-306 in the Italian records). Neither of these kills has been confirmed by the Soviet sources, which instead state that S-32 was in fact sunk on 26 June, probably by CB-2, while only one other submarine (SC-214) was lost during June. A third Italian claim, that CB-4 sank SC-207 on 26 August 1943, is also challenged, but SC-203 was actually lost on that same day.

The successes of the motorboats were limited. Apart from a raid against Soviet landing craft off Sebastopol on 18 June 1942, and damage inflicted on the destroyer *Kharkov* on the night of 2/3 August, the only confirmed success is the sinking of a 3,000-ton cargo ship. Two MAS were destroyed and two others damaged during an air raid on 9 September 1942. MTSM-216 and -210 attacked Soviet vessels without success on 10 and 11 June, but on 13 June MTSM-210 damaged a ferry, which was then sunk by German aircraft. Between May and July 1942 the record shows 65 missions carried out by the MAS boats, 56 by the MTSM and 24 by the midget submarines, all of which were now suffering severely from attrition and hard wear. When autumn of 1942 brought rougher seas they proved unable to remain fully operational, and were sent back to Constanza for the winter.

Late 1942: two 'CB' midget submarines at the Constanza base on the Black Sea coast of Romania, where the *1ᵃ Squadriglia Sommergibili 'CB'* over-wintered. Alone of the Italian Navy contingent, the midget submarines remained in the Black Sea until the Italian surrender in September 1943, although this tour of service highlighted their shortcomings. (AUSSM)

A clearer view of the Caproni 'CB' midget submarine. This photo in fact shows a boat of a later production batch in service with the Xᵃ MAS submarine unit based at Pola in 1944–45. The crew of one of these boats, CB-16, sailed it to Ancona harbour and surrendered to the Allies on 2 October 1944, after killing their commander. (Vitetti)

After the Soviet victory at Stalingrad there was no longer any reason for the Italians to remain in the Black Sea. In March 1943 all the 10th Flotilla craft except MTM-80 were sent back to Italy, while the MAS boats were handed over to the Germans on 20 May after a last mission on the 13th. Only the CB submarines were still operational from Sebastopol, carrying out another 21 missions between June and August 1943, including that which led to the claimed sinking of a Soviet submarine on 26 August. After the Italian surrender on 8 September 1943 the crews joined the Germans, but the midget submarines were left unused in harbour until they were seized by the advancing Soviet forces in August 1944.

Early in 1943 the Italian Navy had planned to acquire another 72 CB boats, cutting the order to 50 that August. Only six of these were actually delivered before the Italian surrender (CB-7 to -12); these formed the *2ᵃ Squadriglia Sommergibili 'CB'* at Taranto, but carried out no missions. After the surrender the damaged CB-7 was seized by the Germans at Pola and cannibalized, and the rest remained in Allied-held Taranto harbour, seeing no use other than training.

* * *

In winter 1941/42, Lts Wolk and Belloni of the 10th MAS had carried out a series of joint exercises with Gamma frogmen and midget submarines. In order to increase both the swimmers' range and the weight of the explosive charges they could carry, it was suggested that a midget submarine might both carry the frogmen close to their targets, and then tow them right underneath their hulls. The idea was tested in Lake Iseo in northern Italy with two modified CA boats; results were satisfactory, and a depth of 47m (154ft) was reached. In spring 1942 the Navy had two more CA boats built specifically for use as Gamma carriers; delivered in 1943, they were slightly modified and with improved capabilities, reaching a depth of 70m (230ft). With the defences of Allied harbours in the Mediterranean now greatly strengthened, other targets were sought; these did not lack ambition, since a plan was devised to attack the harbours of both New York, and Freetown in West Africa (an important Allied shipping hub), from the Italian Atlantic submarine base at Bordeaux. The submarine *Leonardo da Vinci* was adapted to carry a CA boat on its deck; the first trials were troublesome, and the CA still required improvement, but the 'kangaroo' carrying adaptation worked. The mission was planned for December 1943, and while waiting for the new models of CA to be built the *Leonardo da Vinci* reverted to its normal operational role. It was sunk on 25 May 1943, as the Battle of the Atlantic tipped decisively against the Axis submarine forces, and the Italian surrender four months later put paid to the plan.

'SAN MARCO' NAVAL INFANTRY

Origins
The Royal Naval Infantry Corps (*Corpo di Fanteria Real Marina*) was formed after Italy's unification in 1861, to garrison ports and naval arsenals and to provide embarked detachments for warships. Budget restrictions caused its disbandment in 1878, leaving only *compagnie da sbarco*, 'landing parties'. These embarked detachments saw employment in Africa, Crete, and during the 1900 Boxer Rebellion in China.

While the official decree was only issued retrospectively in 1919, a regiment was rebuilt after Italy's entry into World War I in 1915. Together with a *Raggruppamento Artiglieria*, this *Reggimento Marina*, with four battalions, formed a naval brigade. The *Brigata Marina* was employed to defend the lagoon of Venice, and, at the conclusion of the war, to seize the Istrian peninsula and some islands off the Dalmatian coast. Although it was then reduced to a single *Battaglione di Marina*, Venice asked that in celebration of its role during the Great War this unit should be named after the city's patron saint. The king approved the request, and the battalion adopted the name 'San Marco' and the insignia of St Mark's lion on its uniforms.

During the interwar years the battalion was reorganized several times, while officially retaining one artillery and four rifle companies; in 1922, for instance, it numbered 348 all ranks and four 65/17 guns. It was stationed on the eastern shore of the Gulf of Venice at Pola on the Istrian peninsula, formerly the main Austro-Hungarian naval base. Elements were also deployed in China along with some naval vessels, in the Italian settlement at Tzien-Tzin, in Peking and Shanghai. (These latter detachments kept the 'San Marco' insignia, but were subsequently reorganized as the Italian Battalion in China; they would eventually be disarmed by the Japanese in September 1943.)

The 'San Marco' Battalion took part in the last phase of the Italian-Abyssinian war in 1936 and, in April 1939, in the seizure of Albania. The battalion was selective of its personnel, both on physical grounds and also because – given its deployment overseas, particularly in the multinational stations in China – the Navy wanted it to make a good impression when compared with its British, American and Japanese counterparts.

The unit's main mission was still to garrison Pola, and it was not until 1935 that a decision was taken to start intensive training for seaborne landing operations, a task that soon took priority. (This training included rowing – a necessity, given the complete lack of motorized landing craft at that date.) At the same time plans were made to bring the battalion up to a strength of about 1,000 in the event of mobilization, with four rifle and one machine-gun companies. The battalion was mobilized on 15 August 1939, shortly before the outbreak of war in Europe, and early in 1940 it was expanded to a regiment of two battalions, named 'Bafile' and 'Grado'. (Both names had significance from World War I, the former recalling Lt Andrea Bafile, who had been awarded the Gold War Medal of Honour.) In October 1940 it became the marine infantry component of the *Forza Navale da Sbarco*, 'Naval Landing Force'.

Men of the 'San Marco' naval infantry company at the 'Betasom' Italian Atlantic submarine base at Bordeaux, probably in 1940–41; see Plate D1 for reconstruction. (AUSSM)

Italian landing forces

Italy's lack of preparedness to carry out seaborne landing operations can be explained reasonably enough by considering her geo-political situation. Confined to the Mediterranean, the Italian Navy judged that in the event of war with Britain and France the great naval superiority of those powers would make it impossible to maintain supply lines to the colonies of Libya and Ethiopia (Abyssinia). In 1938 Malta was fully recognized as a strategic priority, but even if it could be brought under Italian control this would not have counterbalanced Allied naval superiority. The only realistic coasts for Italian landing operations were judged to be those of the Balkans, Corsica and southern France, and, given the general lack of coastal defences at that time, such operations were anticipated as being largely limited to enemy harbours or undefended shorelines. (Although Japan offers an exception, this was then the conventional wisdom in several countries.)

The fall of France in June 1940, coinciding with Italy's entry into the war, changed the strategic position and revived consideration of plans for seaborne landings. Remarkably, however, the Navy made practically no investment in either the necessary craft or the techniques for their employment. The approach of the Naval Staff – fearful of risking direct confrontation – was distinctly half-hearted. Judging that the British Mediterranean Fleet would react to any landings on British territory within four days, the Staff placed an extraordinary restriction on the planning: naval units would remain in the landing area for just three days, thereafter leaving a landed force practically on its own.

The first seaborne landing to be planned, from August 1940, was the seizure of the Greek island of Corfu. Just before Italy attacked Greece on 28 October, on the 25th, the *Forza Navale Speciale* (FNS) was formed under Vice-Adm Vittorio Tur. This included seven cargo ships to transport elements of one Army infantry division and the 'Bafile' Bn of the 'San Marco' Regt, for a total strength of 4,670 all ranks, 240 horses, and 100 motor vehicles. The plan required the 'Bafile' Bn to land first (a task for which only motor launches were available) and create a beachhead, with the infantry following up only after harbours had been seized. The Corfu operation was first postponed and eventually cancelled, but the FNS was not disbanded. In April 1941 it executed small landings on Corfu and on the Dalmatian coast and islands: the 'Bafile' Bn landed at Krk (Veglia) on 15 April and on Cefalonia on the 30th, and the 'Grado' Bn at Sibenik on 17 April, at Split (Spalato) on the 21st and at Lesina on the 22nd.

The planned assault on Malta

This left only two further plans for seaborne landings: operation 'C 2', the seizure of Corsica in the event of a French defection to rejoin the Allies; and the embryo of plan 'C 3', for an assault on Malta. (These would be followed in July 1942 by plan 'C 4', for the establishment of a beachhead in Tunisia.) Previous plans for landings on Malta dated back to spring 1940, but the prospect was regarded by both the Army and Navy staffs without enthusiasm. Plan 'C' was scuppered by the lack of motor barges, of which only five were available out of the 80 considered necessary. In May 1941 the Navy proposed building some 100 landing craft to be used to establish a beachhead, as part of an assault envisaged as needing some 160–180 transport vessels – about twice the number actually available. In January 1942, at a time of relative naval advantage in the eastern Mediterranean, the proposed operation was raised again by Mussolini during a meeting with Göring, and planning for 'C 3' began in February, although full-scale preparations did not start until April. By then a basic operational plan had emerged from discussions among Italian and German commanders.

Rommel's second attack against Tobruk was due to begin in May 1942, and, unless the Axis forces quickly achieved a decisive victory that opened the road to Alexandria and the Suez Canal, the assault against Malta would follow soon afterwards (the German codename for the airborne phase was 'Herkules'). For 'C 3' the Italian FNS was to be supported by four battleships, ten cruisers and 20 destroyers amongst other vessels; there would be seven main cargo ships, four ferries, 12 main troop transports plus eight others equipped with landing gangways, 65 landing craft (of which only 28 were actually available by mid-July), 100 motor launches (only 58 available), and 245 other vessels, including 81 German assault boats. During June 1942 an assault force of some 100,000 men was assembled. The plan envisaged a joint airborne and seaborne landing on the south-eastern coast of Malta; it hinged on the rapid seizure and prompt availability of Hal Far airfield, in order to protect a main beachhead nearby in St George's Bay (Marsa Sirocco).

C: 'SAN MARCO' NAVAL INFANTRY REGIMENT, 1940–42

(1) *Capitano di corvetta*; Italy, 1940

Navy field service dress copied the Army's grey-green woollen uniform, with a beret as the immediate distinguishing feature; officers favoured finer cloth in a pale shade. This lieutenant-commander's rank insignia are the same as on the blue uniform – one narrow above one wide stripe on his forearm – with the exception of the 'boxed' star on his beret, equivalent to the Army rank of major. 'San Marco' personnel wore pointed-rectangular red lapel patches bearing the gold metal Lion of St Mark insignia (**see detail 1a**) above the national silver star. The ribbons are those of the Navy Bronze Medal, War Valour Cross, Far East Medal (for pre-war service in China), War Merit Cross, War Service Badge, and silver Sports Medal. 'San Marco' personnel carried a dagger, the mark of elite and special forces.

(2) *Marò guastatore*; Libya, 1942

The khaki cotton blouse of the naval infantry tropical uniform had a khaki sailor's collar, with two white edge-stripes and a star in the corners, just as on the blue rig; the double white trim was repeated on the cuffs. The cloth version of the 'San Marco' badge is worn on both cuffs, and the assault engineer's qualification badge on his left sleeve – a wreathed upright sword set on a flaming petard. Khaki cotton trousers were issued, but shorts were very common. The Army M33 steel helmet has a canvas cover. This seaman has one of the so-called 'Samurai' vests, to carry – on both front and back – magazines for the M38A submachine gun, here in its stowage bag.

(3) *Vice capo squadra* attached from Blackshirt MILMART unit; Italy, 1942

Fascist militiamen attached to the 'San Marco' Regt wore their usual Army-style grey-green uniforms and black shirts, but with the Navy beret. Originally this bore a simple anchor badge, but in 1942 they adopted the 'San Marco' lion. They might display the cloth version on both cuffs, or – as here – superimpose their MVSN black 'double flame' patches bearing silver *fasces* over the red lapel patch, leaving the lion showing at the top. This lance-sergeant from an AA machine-gun unit has thin yellow piping around the edge of his 'flames' (though it is too fine to be visible here), and a machine-gun qualification badge below the rank chevrons on his left sleeve. His ribbons are for the East Africa War Badge, War Service Badge, and a Fascist militia seniority cross.

The reinforced attackers would then advance inland to Valletta, and into the north-western tip of the island.

Following the rapid fall of Tobruk on 22 June 1942, and Rommel's subsequent advance into Egypt, the Malta operation was at first postponed, and eventually cancelled on 27 July. The consequences for Rommel's trans-Mediterranean supply lines during the autumn are too well known to need discussion here.

On 5 January 1943 the FNS was disbanded, after having carried out operation 'C 2' – the landing on Corsica – on 11/12 November 1942.

The 'San Marco' Regiment: operations
In October 1940 the 'San Marco' Regt was ready to land on Corfu, strengthened for this purpose by an attached battalion-sized unit of the *Milizia Artiglieria Marittima* (MILMART), the Blackshirt (Fascist militia) coastal artillery. In spite of its title this battalion actually had no artillery pieces, and eventually made up the numbers after the redeployment of one rifle company of the 'San Marco' sent to protect Italy's Atlantic submarine base at Bordeaux.

Following the cancellation of the landing on Corfu there were no missions for the 'San Marco' until April 1941. After the German attack in the Balkans on 6 April, and the Italian invasion of Yugoslavia, the 'Grado' Bn landed on the Dalmatian coast and islands. After seizing Split, Sibenik and Cattaro (Kotor) it was stationed there until autumn, taking part from August 1941 in counter-guerrilla operations in Montenegro. The 'Bafile' Bn was sent to Greece in May 1941, deployed between Patrai and Corinth. Both the 'Bafile' and the 'Grado' were back in central Italy in autumn 1941, being deployed on the Tyrrhenian coast of Tuscany. There, together with Army units and (from January 1942) the *Camicie Nere da Sbarco* battalions (the Blackshirt Fascist militia seaborne landing units), they would spend until the spring of 1942 preparing and practicing for the planned 'C 3' operation against Malta.[3]

North Africa
Late in 1941, after Rommel had advanced into Cyrenaica and laid siege to the Australian-held port of Tobruk, fresh troops were needed on that front, and particularly troops that could be used for seaborne raids behind Allied lines. On 10 November 1941 three companies of the 'San Marco' Regt (two from the 'Bafile' Bn, and the MG company from 'Grado') formed the regiment's new III Bn, with an actual strength of 22 officers, 35 NCOs and 479 rank-and-file. Weapons included 400 rifles, 12× 9mm Beretta submachine guns, 3× 45mm mortars, 12× 8mm heavy machine guns and 16× 47/32 anti-tank guns. Shipped to Libya in mid-November, the unit was deployed on a stretch of the coast, with the intention of carrying out training while providing coastal defence. This coincided with the start on 18 November 1941 of Operation *Crusader*, the British Eighth Army's offensive to relieve Tobruk. The naval battalion was promptly deployed as ordinary infantry in the front line, attached to the 'Sabratha' Infantry Division. Lack of 81mm mortars and the shortage of heavy MGs, not to mention the lack of adequate training, cost the battalion 47 killed in action in addition to numerous wounded, and on 27 December its strength was down to 23 officers, 31 NCOs and 446 rankers.

3 See Elite 99, *Italian Army Elite Units & Special Forces 1940–43*

Summer 1942: naval infantrymen of III Bn, 'San Marco' Regt pulling a 47/32 anti-tank gun through the much-bombed harbour town of Tobruk, Libya. They wear the khaki tropical version of naval uniform with shorts and canvas gaiters, along with Mills-type webbing equipment; the officer has a 'Sahariana' jacket and a pith helmet – see Plate D2. (AUSSM)

In January 1942 the battalion took part in Rommel's second advance into Cyrenaica; on 22 January, III Bn was at Agedabia, reaching Antelat on the 25th. It remained there in garrison until transferred to Benghazi on 7 March, now with the task of coastal and harbour defence. It was planned to send the unit back to Italy, and one company had already flown out, when, under command of the *Deutsches Afrikakorps*, the remainder were selected for a seaborne landing behind the Eighth Army's defence line at Gazala; this mission was planned to coincide with Rommel's new offensive in May 1942. The battalion moved to the Gulf of Bomba on 11 May, but the landing was cancelled; instead the unit was put under command of Italian X Corps and was deployed in June to Tmimi, to defend the coast road.

When the South African defence of Tobruk collapsed, III Bn was among those units that entered the perimeter on 22 June and, after the German breakthrough, occupied the town and harbour (they also took liberal

A group of 'San Marco' *guastatori* assault engineers in North Africa, 1942. They pose wearing the tropical version of the blouse and various types of shorts, along with full equipment including 9mm Beretta M38A submachine guns in canvas cases, and 'Samurai' ammunition vests for the magazines – see Plate C2. These men are probably among those who were earmarked for the cancelled raid behind the British Gazala Line. (AUSSM)

advantage of the captured South African and British stores depots). Apart from a small group of 45 all ranks who were detached and sent to Mersa Matruh in Egypt, the rest of the battalion was retained in Tobruk for garrison and coastal defence tasks. Only the HQ and the services were in the town itself; the rest of the battalion were deployed along a 12km (7.5 mile) stretch of coastline extending on both sides of the town, mostly in small strongpoints formed around a single heavy MG or an AT gun. These little groups suffered from isolation and lack of adequate communications, and had to be re-supplied with food and water every two days.

In the night of 14 September 1942, the British 'Force A' (elements of 11 Royal Marine Commando) and 'Force B' (D Co, 1st Bn Argyll & Sutherland Highlanders) landed at Tobruk as part of Operation *Agreement*, which also involved an advance from inland by parties from the Long Range Desert Group and Special Air Service. The 'big raid' was aimed at the harbour and the main airfields, but the Commandos were landed 2 miles east of their intended site. They consequently ran into two of the small 'San Marco' outposts, provoking an unexpectedly prompt and vigorous reaction. Facing this threat from the sea, the battalion commander gathered together all available men including those from the HQ and service elements, and sent the cadres of the two companies to counterattack the Commandos near Mengar el Auda west of Tobruk, and the Argylls at Mersa Sciausc east of the town. The raid from inland was also driven off, and at dawn the Commandos and Highlanders had no option but to surrender. The III/'San Marco' suffered about a dozen casualties of the total of 15 Italians killed and 43 wounded in this action. In recognition of its conduct III Bn then acquired the name 'Tobruch' (the Italian spelling).

After the defeat of the Axis forces at El Alamein in October and the withdrawal at first from Egypt and then from Cyrenaica, the 'Tobruch' Bn remained in the port as a rearguard until the place was evacuated on 13 November. It was then withdrawn westwards, at first to Mersa el Brega, then to Buerat, eventually leaving the Libyan capital Tripoli on 21 January 1943. Now attached to the 'La Spezia' Inf Div, it fell back to the Mareth Line in Tunisia.

Tunisia, winter 1942–43: the commanding officer of the 'San Marco' Regt (centre) wears naval grey-green uniform, with a beret bearing the three 'boxed' stars of *capitano di vascello*, equivalent to full colonel. The regimental collar patches are butted tight against the national star on his collar; note naval cuff ranking, and transverse shoulder tabs. (Right) are admirals in naval blues. (Left) is the commander of the Blackshirt militia unit attached to the regiment, still wearing the pre-war Army-style uniform in pale grey-green with black trouser-stripes and gold cuff ranking; on his lapels he wears the 'San Marco' patch above the black MVSN 'flames' with gold metal *fasces*. (AUSSM)

Tunis, winter 1942–43: a 'San Marco' naval infantryman, wearing the khaki tropical version of the naval blouse with white trim over a turtleneck pullover, poses with a veteran German soldier from the replacement unit *Tunis Feld-Bataillon 1* in the Bizerta beachhead. (Cappellano)

The rest of the 'San Marco' Regt had meanwhile continued to train along with other units for the Malta assault, until the plan was called off in late July 1942. Following the Allied invasion of French North-West Africa on 8 November 1942, the 'San Marco' took part alongside Army units in the long-planned landing on Corsica. This operation on 11–12 November was unopposed, and the regiment was almost immediately transferred to Tunisia, arriving during 20–24 November. At this time the 'San Marco' comprised the regimental HQ company, a company from the MILMART and a smoke-laying platoon; the 'Bafile' Bn (HQ Co, four rifle companies, 81mm mortar company, 47/32 AT gun and MILMART company); the 'Grado' Bn (same organization minus the mortar company); and the III 'Tobruch' Bn withdrawing from Cyrenaica (three rifle and one 45mm mortar companies). A newly formed IV 'Caorle' Bn (four rifle companies) was still in Italy and destined for southern France. Other units included the 'N' and 'P' battalions (see below), also bound for southern France, and the company at the Bordeaux submarine base.

The 'San Marco' Regt with the 'Grado' and 'Bafile' Bns (plus one company from the 'N' Bn) landed at Bizerta north of Tunis, to build a beachhead along with other Italian and German units. The regiment had an overall strength of about 3,200 all ranks. Given the threat of the Allied advance from Algeria the battalions were deployed separately, sometimes broken down into sub-units to face as many of the Allied spearheads as possible. On 1 December the MILMART company attached to the 'Grado' Bn was used to reinforce a German detachment, fighting the regiment's first action of the Tunisian campaign against British paratroopers at Pont du Fahs; two of the Blackshirts earned Iron Crosses. While the 'Bafile' Bn was deployed for coastal defence, the 'Grado' was ordered on 22 January 1943 to mount a counterattack on the Djebel Bou Dabouss massif; it retook this feature, capturing 200 prisoners at the cost of 24 killed and 65 wounded.

The crew of a 47/32 anti-tank gun of the 'Grado' Bn in Tunisia, spring 1943. All are wearing the sailor's tropical blouse, with the 'San Marco' patch on the cuffs below the double white trim. They have been issued long khaki cotton trousers; note that they still have the Mills-type webbing equipment, and the gun commander has a hessian helmet-cover. (Crociani)

Following the withdrawal into Tunisia of the 'Tobruch' Bn, the 'San Marco' Regt was able for the first time to reunite all its units and, after a period of rest (and rebuilding with untrained sailors from the naval bases), it went back into the front line. The 'Tobruch' was deployed on the Mareth Line and took part on 5–6 April 1943 in the battle of Wadi Akarit. Now reduced to fewer than 100 men, it was pulled out of the line, and on 14 April the survivors were sent back to Italy by air.

Also facing the Allied offensive in April 1943, the 'Grado' Bn was compelled to withdraw from Djebel Bou Dabouss, losing 150 men in the process, and on 29 April it acted as a rearguard for the German withdrawal to Lake Garaet Achkel west of Bizerta. On 4 May the 'Grado' joined the regimental HQ and the 'Bafile' Bn at Bizerta, where all eventually surrendered to the Allied forces on 9 May. Only 105 men garrisoning the island of La Galite escaped capture, being evacuated on 12 May by Italian MAS boats.

The now-skeletal remnants of the 'San Marco' Regt were dispersed between France and Italy. In November–December 1942 the IV 'Caorle' Bn had been deployed to Toulon in southern France, while the company protecting the submarine base at Bordeaux had been reinforced by a newly formed second company. Another company was in Rome, protecting the Naval Staff HQ, while new recruits and the regimental depot were spread along the northern Adriatic coast between Venice and Pola.

The fate of these units in the days following the Italian surrender in September 1943 is in many cases uncertain. Facing the German reaction, most of the men had to choose between surrender and internment by the Germans, or co-operation with them; the only ones to escape this stark choice were the company in Rome and some two-thirds of the men deployed at Pola, who were able to make for their homes. For the others it was now a choice between joining the Germans; fighting against them alongside the partisans; or, for the lucky ones who managed to make their way to Allied-occupied southern Italy, returning to the ranks of the *Regia Marina*.

The 'P', 'N' and 'NP' special forces

The 'San Marco' Regt also had under command special forces units specifically conceived for sabotage missions, in expectation of the planned assault on Malta by the *Forza Navale Speciale*. In March 1941 a first group of volunteers from the 'San Marco' Regt were sent to the parachute school at Tarquinia; it was originally intended that they should be employed in Greece, to seize the Corinth Canal crossings. From the first three officers and 50 men they gradually developed into a full unit for sabotage missions; the single company of March 1941 was augmented by numerous volunteers, to become a 340-strong battalion with HQ services and three companies. Formed in March 1942, the **'P' Battalion** (for *Paracadutisti*, paratroopers) continued to train intensively on the steep cliffs of the

Tyrrhenian coast, similar to those on the southern shore of Malta. The men of both the 'P' and 'N' (see below) battalions were trained for parachute drops into the sea with special inflatable boats, which they would use to approach the south-eastern coast of Malta, infiltrating to sabotage key targets before the first assault wave landed. This latter, composed of one battalion of the 'San Marco' Regt and one Blackshirt landing battalion, was to establish a beachhead for the following infantry units.

After the Malta assault was cancelled the 'P' Bn was deployed as ordinary infantry; in January 1943 it was sent to garrison Toulon, the main French naval base in the Mediterranean, but in February it was pulled back to Italy, at first to Livorno and then to Tarquinia. Following the Allied *Torch* landings in French NW Africa and the Axis establishment of the Tunisian beachhead, the Axis forces there faced an increased need for manpower; the specialists of 'P' Bn were of little value as conventional infantry, given their low strength and unusual training, but they might still be used to carry out sabotage missions behind Allied lines. New training courses for sabotage and commando-style missions were then started at Tarquinia and at nearby Civitavecchia, with the unit broken down into small squads of one officer and 13–15 men each. They were also trained as 'tank hunters'. On 1 April 1943 the 'P' Bn was finally merged with the 'N' Bn, to form the *Gruppo Battaglioni 'NP'* (Swimmer-Paratrooper Battalion Group).

Following the Axis occupation of Vichy France in response to the Allied landings in French North Africa, paratroopers of the 'San Marco' Regt's parachute battalion parade in Toulon in January 1943, behind their magnificent red and gold banner bearing the winged lion of Venice, with four streaming 'flames'. Note the 'Samurai' ammo vests, and the white fleece lining showing at the top of the leather gloves; under their overcoats they wear the same uniform as illustrated in Plate D3. (Vitetti)

Ready for a jump, this swimmer/parachutist of the 'NP' Bn is photographed with equipment pioneered by the 'N' Bn before the amalgamation of the swimmer and parachutist special units of the 'San Marco' Regiment. He wears a paratroop helmet, a short-sleeved swimming suit and flippers. Under his right arm can be seen the inflatable mattress used to support him and his kit during his swim to shore. Weapons, explosives and other equipment were carried in a separate waterproof bag that was detached to hang on a rope as soon as the parachute opened. (Vitetti)

The **'N' Battalion** (for *Nuotatori*, swimmers) had its origins in a group of 50 *guastatori* (assault engineers) put together by the Navy in June 1941 for sabotage operations; this initial *Reparto G* (Guastatori Unit) also included Army personnel. In the planned Malta operation the assault engineers were intended to swim ashore by stealth, and attack targets before the first assault wave landed. These hand-picked men were trained under the supervision of the Gamma group of the 10th MAS Flotilla, to swim and use inflatable swimming aids. The initial group was strengthened with volunteers from the 'San Marco' Regt and from the MVSN (Blackshirts), eventually reaching a strength of 200. On 21 June 1942 these formed the *Battaglione 'Mazzucchelli'* (named after a World War I hero), soon redesignated *Battaglione 'N'*.

A senior NCO and a seaman of the 'NP' Bn of the 'San Marco' Regiment. The second chief petty officer (left) wears Army-style uniform, with gold sleeve chevrons and 'San Marco' collar patches. The *marò* – a term used for both sailors and marines – wears naval 'square rig', with the battalion's new qualification brevet on his left sleeve – see Plate D3a. (Vitetti)

On the night of 4/5 September an officer and 14 men were carried by motorboat to land behind the El Alamein Line, with the aim of sabotaging both the aqueduct and the railway line that served the British forward positions. Lacking adequate briefing, the party were unable to find the aqueduct, but managed to reach and destroy a portion of the railway. Unable to make their way back to Axis lines over land, as intended, all were taken prisoner (though the commander would manage to escape, at the third attempt).

In November 1942 the second of the battalion's five companies was sent to Tunisia. The rest of the unit was first employed at Bastia during the seizure of Corsica, and then, at the end of that month, was transferred from Livorno to southern France. Deployed at first at Hyères, it subsequently moved to Toulon along with the 'P' Bn, following it back to Italy in February 1943. In Tunisia, the 2nd Company could not, in the event, be employed as a formed unit in the intended seaborne commando-style role, due to the unsuitability of the sea conditions and the coastal terrain. In March 1943 all the companies

1

3a

3

2

were therefore split up, each into ten squads of one officer, one NCO and eight rankers, with the same role in mind. In late July 1943 the battalion's 3rd Co was deployed to Sicily and attached to the 'Assietta' Infantry Division.

On 1 April 1943 the combined **'NP' Battalion** was created in Italy, and at the end of May it counted some 580 swimmers and 240 paratroopers. Italy was now directly threatened by Allied invasion; given the uncertainty over the possible landing areas, parts of the battalion were sent to both Sicily and Sardinia, along with Army special forces of the X Arditi Regiment.[4] The plan was to use them in small groups, partly dressed in civilian clothes; they were to hide up and let Allied troops advance past them, before emerging to use pre-placed weapons and explosives caches to carry out sabotage missions and guerrilla warfare behind Allied lines.

Ten 'NP' squads were sent to Sardinia, where they remained inactive until Italy's surrender in September 1943. Seven other squads were sent to Sicily, following the earlier deployment there of 3rd Co from 'N' Battalion. The sabotage squads had neither the time nor the opportunity to prepare the ordnance caches that had been envisaged. They were eventually landed from motorboats behind the Allied lines in eastern Sicily, where they carried out a few sabotage missions in late July and early August 1943. The remnants of the 'NP' Bn were then evacuated to the Italian mainland a few weeks before the September surrender.

AIR FORCE SPECIAL FORCES

The birth of the Air Force special forces was also prompted by the plan to assault Malta, although in their case only very late in the day. This was due to the belated decision to include in the plan the rapid seizure and preparation of Hal Far airfield in order to bring in air-landing troops of the 'La Spezia' Division.

4 See Elite 99, *Italian Army Elite Units & Special Forces 1940–43*

Probably photographed at Tarquinia in summer 1942, Air Force paratroopers pose with an Air Force lieutenant pilot wearing the blue-grey service uniform. The *paracadutisti* wear the Army-style khaki tropical paratroop uniform, with Air Force beret and lapel patches – see Plate E1. On the upper left sleeve is the badge then worn by all qualified paratoopers, and below it the qualification badge of the *Arditi* assault troops. (Vitetti)

The *1° Reparto Paracadutisti della Regia Aeronautica* (1st Air Force Paratroop Unit), tasked with capturing Hal Far, was formed only on 12 May 1942 at Tarquinia, under command of LtCol Edvino Dalmas. Entirely composed of volunteers, it had an HQ (5 officers, 4 NCOs, 20 rankers), and ten squads each with an officer, 2 NCOs and 25 rankers. Most were armed with the standard 6.5mm Mannlicher-Carcano M91 carbine, the officers and NCOs with the 9mm Beretta M38A submachine gun, and their intensive training included the use of explosives and sabotage techniques. Part of the unit was made up of technical specialists tasked with returning the airfield facilities to serviceable condition as soon as possible.

Close-up of an Air Force paratrooper, showing the helmet, the mouse-grey early jump-smock worn before the introduction of the three-colour camouflage version, and part of a Breda 30 squad light machine gun. (Crociani)

Since this latter was a key part of the overall plan, on 10 June 1942 another unit was formed, at Cameri airfield near Novara, specifically tasked with this role. This *Battaglione 'Loreto'* was intended both to take part in the restoration of facilities at Hal Far and to garrison and defend it. Its first two companies were to be deployed in defence. The 1st Co had 6 officers, 17 NCOs and 172 airmen, being composed of one machine-gun platoon armed with 20mm AA cannon, and three light machine-gun platoons. The 2nd Co had 5 officers, 12 NCOs and 200 airmen. Officers and NCOs were equipped with SMGs, most others with the M91 carbine. The 3rd Co, responsible for the technical services, comprised 8 officers, 9 NCOs and 199 airmen, one-quarter of them technicians. The 4th Co, responsible for logistics and administration, had 8 officers, 14 NCOs and 185 airmen, again one-quarter of them technicians.

1st Air Force Assault Regiment 'Amedeo d'Aosta'

After the decision to cancel the invasion of Malta the Air Force paratroop unit moved to Arezzo, Tuscany, in late summer 1942. Most of the personnel were granted leave, and the unit was almost forgotten until November, when the Allied *Torch* landings in Morocco and Algeria concentrated the minds of the high command. Both the 1st Paratroop Unit and the 'Loreto' Bn were sent at first to Sicily; and there, on 16 November at Marsala, these units were merged to form the *1° Reggimento d'Assalto della Regia Aeronautica 'Amedeo d'Aosta'* (1st Air Force Assault Regiment 'Amedeo d'Aosta' – named after the Air Force general who had been Viceroy of Ethiopia). The regiment had its own HQ and the newly redesignated 1st Paratroop Bn, and was also originally intended to include the *Battaglione Arditi Distruttori della Regia Aeronautica* (ADRA). This Air Force Assault Engineer Bn, which was still forming, would eventually be an independent unit.

On that same day the Paratroop Bn, only 241 strong, landed in Tunisia. After a short pause at Bizerta, where three of its ten squads were left, it was

---

E

AIR FORCE SPECIAL UNITS; ITALY, 1942

(1) *Tenente*, Air Force Assault Engineer Battalion (ADRA)
This is the khaki cotton version of the typical collarless jacket of Italian special forces, otherwise cut like the 'Sahariana'. Note the matching beret, wide paratrooper's trousers and black jump-boots; an officer's 'Sam Browne' belt with Beretta M34 holster; and the special forces dagger. In the *Regia Aeronautica* only special forces wore the beret; it bears the Air Force officer's cap badge of a crown over a wreathed eagle in gold, on grey-blue backing, and the two stars of his rank. The lieutenant's two rank stripes in gold on grey-blue, the upper one with a diamond-shaped 'curl', are worn on the cuff, but the other insignia are all of Army type. Blue paratroop lapel patches bear the *guastatori* symbol of a winged sword set on a flaming petard, above the national silver star. On his left breast he wears the Air Force's 1942 gold metal parachutist's 'wings'. On the left sleeve is the badge then worn by all qualified paratroopers, above the wreathed sword badge of a qualified *Ardito* assault trooper. The ribbons are those of the Air Force Silver Medal, War Merit Cross, and 2 Years' War Service Badge.

(1a) Metal breast badge of the *Arditi Distruttori Regia Aeronautica* (ADRA).

(2) *Paracadutista*, 1st Air Force Parachute Battalion
Over blue-grey *Regia Aeronautica* uniform he wears the standard Army paratroop helmet with camouflaged cover, a camouflaged jump-smock, a narrower version of the 'Samurai' ammo vest (so as not to interfere with the parachute harness), knee pads and jump-boots. His Beretta M38A SMG is carried in a canvas case secured to his waist by a 10m (c.30ft) rope, and at the ankle by a sleeve. When his parachute opens he will lift the muzzle out of the ankle sleeve and lower the case to dangle below him until he lands. (To hit the ground with it still stowed as illustrated would obviously result in broken bones.)

(3) *Primo aviere*, 'Loreto' Battalion
This corporal carrying a Breda 30 'automatic rifle' (light machine gun), photographed while lined up for inspection, wears surprisingly inadequate equipment: a greenish-painted Army belt with a single rifle cartridge pouch and a bayonet, but neither the neck support sling, nor the cleaning-kit pouch and pistol prescribed for an LMG crew 'No.1'. The battalion received these Czech steel helmets, painted blue-grey with a black Air Force stencil. Otherwise he wears standard Air Force blue-grey service uniform, with bright blue collar patches. On the left sleeve above his red rank chevrons is this battalion's yellow sword-and-wings badge.

A NCO and airmen of the 'Loreto' Bn drawn up for inspection – see Plate E3. Note battalion badge above the rank chevrons on the left sleeve; and the Czechoslovakian steel helmet, issued to this unit to make up for a shortage of Italian M33 helmets in Air Force stores. (Crociani)

deployed westwards to face the advancing US and British forces. On the evening of 20 November the understrength battalion, along with the German Paratroop Engineer Bn 'Witzig', was deployed on the Djebel Abjod close to the Algerian border. The following day both German and Italian paratroopers attacked the advancing British forces, taking them by surprise, but soon faced strong counterattacks. Out of 81 men the Italians lost 4 killed, 7 wounded and abandoned, and 44 missing; LtCol Dalmas was also wounded, but was evacuated to Italy. Reinforced by the three squads from Bizerta on 23 November, the paratroopers held their positions until the 25th when, under heavy artillery fire, both Germans and Italians withdrew some 50km (31 miles) eastwards. What was left of the Air Force Paratroop Bn was then deployed in rear areas, to defend the airfields of Tunis, Gabes and Sfax against Allied raids.

The first two companies of the 'Loreto' Bn were shipped from Sicily to Tunis aboard destroyers on 15 January 1943; the 3rd and 4th Cos were left in Sicily to repair airfields (in May they would be moved to Sardinia to carry out the same duties). At the same time the new commanding officer of the 1st Air Force Assault Regt arrived in Tunisia; he found that the unit had been reduced to 6 of the original 11 officers, 12 NCOs out of 28, and 174 airmen out of 274. He requested replacements for men, weapons and equipment before the unit could again be employed as infantry (the paratroopers had even been sent to Tunisia without steel helmets).

His request was only answered when the situation worsened still further; in April 1943 elements of both the Paratroop and 'Loreto' battalions were regrouped and reinforced using spare Air Force personnel, to be deployed at Enfidaville under the Italian First Army. At this time the regiment had an HQ company; the Paratroop Bn with three companies (the first two mainly paratroopers, the MG Co made up with new Air Force personnel); and the 'Loreto' Bn with four companies (again, the first two from the original unit, the others from new personnel) – armed with a few more SMGs, but still with only (on paper) 18 MGs and 42 LMGs. Attached to the 'Pistoia' Inf Div, the cobbled-together regiment fought until the end, at Wadi Akarit and Enfidaville, until it surrendered in May near Mateur. On 2 July 1943 the regiment was practically disbanded, leaving cadres only. On the 23rd it was re-formed on paper, to a reduced strength and with undetermined tasks, though theoretically to conduct guerrilla warfare against the Allied forces landing in Sicily.

'ADRA' Battalion

The *Battaglione Arditi Distruttori della Regia Aeronautica* (ADRA), Air Force Assault Engineer Bn, had officially been formed as part of the 1st Air Force Assault Regt on 10 December 1942, but its composition was only defined on 25 January 1943. It was to have an HQ and three companies, each with three platoons, each having 2 officers, 3 NCOs and 24 rank-and-file. These formed squads each with an NCO and 8 rankers.

Their objectives were broadly defined as enemy airfield facilities, fuel and ammunition depots. The approach to the targets might be by either parachute, land or sea. Courses had begun at Tarquinia in September 1942, but the belated recruitment of volunteers, the time needed to train them, and delays in the delivery of weapons and equipment, meant that the first 60 Arditi were not available until April 1943, when the bulk of the 1st Air Force Assault Regt was already in Tunisia. As a consequence, on 10 April 1943 the 'ADRA' Bn was detached and made independent.

Its baptism of fire came in June 1943, when it took part in a mass sabotage operation against Allied airfields in North Africa. Ten 'ADRA' patrols, along with parties from the Army's X Arditi (see Elite 99), were flown from bases in Italy, France and Greece, only to land in most cases far from their targets. As a consequence of faulty intelligence many of these had not been studied properly, or were badly chosen (some were no longer even in use). Most of the patrols were taken prisoner hours, or at best days, after landing, and without reaching their targets. The exception was one patrol dropped in Cyrenaica which, chased by British forces and down to just two men, managed on the night of 17/18 June to penetrate Benina airfield and destroy or damage (amongst others) two USAAF B-24 Liberator bombers and two RAF Wellington bombers. The two Arditi eventually surrendered.

ABOVE
An *ardito* of the *Arditi Distruttori della Regia Aeronautica* battalion posing with parachute and full equipment. On his belly is a small parachute pack attached to the two explosives containers under his arms; after jumping he will release these, hoping that they land close to him. Note also on his right leg the Beretta SMG in a drop bag, which will be released to hang on a rope during the jump – see Plate E2. (Cappellano)

A light machine gun team of the ADRA battalion practising during spring 1943. Note that they both have slung across their backs Beretta SMGs in modified drop bags, with two triple magazine pouches attached. (Vitetti)

BORGHESE AND THE Xᵃ MAS UNITS, 1943–45

The Italian surrender

Italy's surrender on 8 September 1943 saw the bulk of its fleet surrendering at Malta, apart from some minor vessels left in the harbours of northern Italy under German control. The country and its armed forces were split in two, with those in central and northern Italy fighting alongside the Germans under the flag of Mussolini's *Repubblica Sociale Italiana* (RSI, Italian Social Republic), and those in the Allied-controlled south carrying the flag of the Italian kingdom.

The Navy special assault forces were also divided. In the south a new formation was created, the *Mariassalto*, under the command of Capt Forza, but shortage of men and equipment hampered any further development. Recovering the available '*barchini*' and manning them with ex-POWs freed by the Allies, *Mariassalto* performed only a few missions. In January 1944 an attack against German ships at Crete was aborted, but in the spring motorboats were used to land agents in Albania. Two missions employed British 'Chariots', the equivalent of the 'hog' manned torpedoes. On 21 June 1944 the heavy cruiser *Bolzano* was badly holed by 'Chariots' at La Spezia, and on 19 April 1945 the incomplete aircraft carrier *Aquila* was also damaged. In both cases the ships were prevented from sinking by the Germans.

The RSI Navy special assault forces

In the north, at La Spezia, the 10th MAS Flotilla under command of Junio Valerio Borghese reacted with determination to the widespread collapse of the Italian forces, and to the consequent German imprisonment and deportation to Germany of Italian soldiers. The flotilla's barracks at La Spezia never hauled down the Italian flag, and, on 12 September, Borghese was able to reach an agreement with the local Kriegsmarine commander that made the survival of the unit possible, albeit under German control. About half of its personnel, some 200 men, dissented, and were sent home on 'permanent leave'. In September–October 1943 the new *Xᵃ Flottiglia MAS* rebuilt its naval assault force at La Spezia (this Roman form of the ordinal number was widely used in 1943–45). This was done with the explicit consent of Adm Karl Dönitz, the commander-in-chief of the Kriegsmarine, who took a keen interest in the unit, and granted Cdr Borghese a personal interview in October.

The first element to be rebuilt was the surface assault unit, now called *Reparto mezzi d'assalto di superficie 'Vittorio Moccagatta'*; this included the training school – *Gruppo 'Salvatore Todaro'* – which moved from La Spezia to Sesto Calende. The frogman school also moved, first to Portofino and then close to Pola. The manned torpedo and Gamma groups moved from Livorno at first to La Spezia, then to Valdagno. A good many craft were available: about ten '*maiali*', plus a dozen of the new *Siluro San Bartolomeo* type; 35 MTM '*barchini*', plus 25 MTSM and MTSMA torpedo motorboats. In December four CB midget submarines, which had been delivered in September 1943 and seized by the Germans, formed the bulk of a new *Gruppo Sommergibili* to be based at Pola, and six more would become available before the end of the war. This inventory, and the relative ease of production of light craft, soon allowed new developments.

In January 1944 the *Base operativa sud* (Operational Base South) was created at Terracina south of Rome, while the *Base operativa collegamento* (Operational Liaison Base) was established at La Spezia for sabotage and espionage missions. Also in January, three available MAS boats were used to create the *Squadriglia MAS Castagnacci*, which received five more boats later that year. Following the Allied advance up Italy in May–June 1944 after the fall of Cassino, and the landings in southern France in August 1944, on 19 August the X^a MAS organized the 'Mataluno Column'; by 24 August this had driven overland from Sesto Calende to Villefranche (2km from Nice) with ten MTM and ten MTSMA boats, establishing Operational Base West. In February 1945 an Operational Base East was also established on the Istrian peninsula.

Frogmen of the X^a MAS 'NP' Bn during training at their new base at Portofino; this angle shows the shoulder and waist straps of the breathing apparatus. (Vitetti)

Operations

Although carrying out different kinds of operations from those executed before September 1943, the assault craft of the X^a MAS were still quite active.

On 17/18 and 19/20 January 1944 the MTSMA torpedo motorboats had to abort two missions to attack shipping in Naples harbour (one MTSMA was lost due to collision). When the Allies landed at Anzio on 22 January one of the first reactions was a failed attack on vessels off the beachhead on the night of the 22nd/23rd by three MTSMA. On 14 February a motorized column brought to Fiumicino, at the mouth of the River Tiber, five MTSMA and eight MTSM. The '*barchini*' were sent back to La Spezia, and on 20/21 February three of these again attacked the beachhead, sinking the USS motorboat PC-545 and damaging the minesweeper USS *Pioneer*. Other attacks followed, though with heavy losses and no results (22/23 February, two motorboats lost out of three; 23rd/24th, one lost out of two; 24th/25th, five used, no results but no losses).

An assault boat of the MTSMA type; three of these attempted to attack Allied shipping off the Anzio beachhead on the night of 22/23 January 1944, within a matter of hours of the initial landings. In May the X^a MAS surface assault craft were transferred to Sesto Calende – where the 'storm boat' personnel of the German *Lehrkommando 600* were also trained, although segregated in separate quarters. (Molinari)

An MTM 'barchino' of the Xª MAS, probably at the San Remo 'Base West' in autumn 1944. The framing around the bow is the 'palmola', which triggered the initial sinking charge when the boat struck its target. The crewman wears a working overall; the uniform of these Xª MAS units was the grey-green beret, collarless jacket and trousers, setting them apart from the rest of the Navy in traditional 'blues'. (Vitetti)

On 1 March 1944 the MAS squadron at Porto Santo Stefano started its own missions, all without results apart from the first actual engagement on 19 March. Three boats attacked on 1, 3 and 5 March, one on 9 and 14 March. Daily missions were also carried out by one or two MAS in the period 3 to 12 April, one being lost; four MAS were again at sea on 21/22 March, two being lost; but only on the 24th/25th was the sinking of a cargo ship claimed, at the cost of the single MAS engaged. Another MAS out of two employed was sunk on 29/30 March. At the end of April the MAS squadron moved back to Marina di Pisa.

On 13 April the other assault motorboats were back in action, and one out of three boats was lost while claiming the (never confirmed) sinking of a corvette. On 20/21 April they sank the US LST 305 (a success often credited to the Germans), but no result was achieved in an action on the 27th/28th. From 4 June, Base South was evacuated, having suffered a total loss of six MTSM, ten MTSMA and three MAS. In June the MAS moved to Lerici, then to San Remo. On 24 August the first operation was carried out from Base West at Villefranche, which had at first two MTSMA soon followed by ten others, plus ten MTSM. On 25 August a destroyer was probably hit, but the damage could not be confirmed. On the 30th the base moved to San Remo; activity was now greatly hampered by Allied air attacks, and achievements were sparse.

On 16/17 April 1945 seven motorboats heavily damaged the French destroyer *Trombe*, but on the 24th the final mission was carried out, and the following day all the craft were destroyed. The 'hogs' only carried out a single aborted mission, while the Gamma and other underwater units and frogmen (from the 'NP' and 'Vega' battalions) were mainly employed in taking saboteurs and agents behind the Allied lines. A daring mission was carried out on 13/14 April 1945, when two MTSMA from Base East brought agents close to the harbour of Ancona. In most cases, however, the saboteurs and agents were caught by the Allied security forces 'with their feet still wet'.

THE Xª MAS NAVAL INFANTRY

In September 1943 what was left of the 'San Marco' Regt included some 1,000 recruits being trained at the regimental depot at Pola; another thousand-odd with the IV 'Caorle' Bn in southern France; a few hundred of the 'NP' Bn (many still in training) in central Italy and Sardinia; the 350 men of the two companies at Bordeaux, and the 100 in Rome protecting the Naval HQ. Of these roughly 3,200 men, only about 100 from the 'Caorle' Bn, plus most of those at Bordeaux and most of the 'NP', joined the Germans to fight against the Allies; the rest were either taken prisoner by the Germans, or made good their escape to their homes. In spite of the almost complete disappearance of the 'San Marco' units after the surrender, the name and its symbols survived on both sides of the front lines, being coveted for their traditional prestige.

In Allied-controlled Italy, on 1 November 1943 the Navy first rebuilt the 'San Marco' as the *Brigata Marina*, from both Army and Navy personnel, and this unit reverted to the old name on 1 January 1944. Deployed at the front with the Italian Liberation Corps in April 1944, the 'San Marco' and its sub-units (the rebuilt 'Bafile' and 'Grado' battalions) were employed as ordinary infantry. In late 1944 it formed, together with the likewise rebuilt 'Nembo' Parachute Regt, the 'Folgore' Combat Group that took part in the last offensive on the Italian front in April 1945. (These latter units are not to be confused with the 'Folgore' Regt and 'Nembo' Bn rebuilt by the RSI forces, as a parallel exercise in perpetuating famous titles.)

* * *

In German-occupied northern Italy, Cdr Borghese's *Xª Flottiglia MAS* quickly proved a magnet for disbanded military personnel who wished to continue the fight against the Allies, but were reluctant to do so under German command. On 8 September 1943 the flotilla had about 400 men at La Spezia, joined ten days later by another 350 gathered at Pola by LtCdr Umberto Bardelli. By mid-October the naval engineer Capt Nino Buttazzoni had gathered at Viterbo some 50 members of the 'NP' Bn, who also joined the Xª MAS. At this point Borghese's relative independence from the Germans attracted many more volunteers – including Army paratroopers, Arditi, and members of the Fascist militia – and recruitment increased steadily.

Summer 1944: *Capitano di Fregata* Borghese in conversation with *Capitano di Fregata* Luigi Carallo, commander of the *Divisione Decima* until his death that December. Carallo displays on his left sleeve the '*Arditi*' badge above the metal Xª MAS shield. (Vitetti)

Three men from the 'NP' Bn pose shortly after joining the Xª MAS Flotilla in autumn 1943. The left and right-hand sailors display on the 'San Marco' lapel patches provisional embroidered versions of the RSI wreathed *gladius*, while the middle one has, for some reason, a larger version of the outdated national stars. The man on the left wears the 'NP' qualification brevet on his left breast pocket. (Molinari)

On 27 October 1943, Buttazzoni formed under Borghese's command a new *Battaglione 'NP'* with an HQ and two, later three companies. Intended for sabotage and espionage behind Allied lines, the battalion was sent for training to Iesolo, where a 4th (Mortar) Co was formed in December 1943–January 1944; this was followed by a 5th (Heavy Weapons) Company. Sabotage specialists were grouped into a separate company, to be carried by CB midget submarines. A first mission failed, the group of four being immediately captured and – since they were in disguise – shot by the Allies.

In November 1943, Borghese formed another battalion, at first named 'Maestrale' and then 'Barbarigo' (named after warships), with an HQ and four rifle companies under command of LtCdr Bardelli. The aim was to form two naval infantry regiments, one for field operations and one for garrison duties, but both adopting the insignia of the old 'San Marco' Regiment. In November and December 1943, Borghese's Xª MAS Flotilla already boasted 800–1,000 naval infantry – an autonomous force strong enough to attract attention.

(Confusingly contradictory though it seems, for the rest of the war the increasing numbers of infantry units formed under Borghese's sponsorship, eventually amounting to a small division and absorbing the majority of the RSI Navy's personnel, would continue to claim the affiliation and display insignia of what had originally been a single naval tactical unit – the famous 10th Torpedo Motorboat Flotilla.)

On 4 November 1943, Cdr Borghese was appointed Deputy Chief of Naval Staff (Operations), but he would soon find himself in confrontation with the RSI's new Undersecretary of State for the Navy, Cdr Ferruccio Ferrini. The latter's plans to rebuild some kind of an RSI Navy were opposed by Adm Dönitz, since the German partiality towards Borghese made the

Xª MAS FLOTILLA; ITALY, 1944

(1) *Guardiamarina*, 'Barbarigo' Battalion; Anzio, early 1944

This first naval infantry battalion of the Xª MAS Flotilla wore uniforms and insignia that were to become typical of this organization as it expanded to divisional size. The single stripe with a round 'curl', identifying the Navy's lowest commissioned rank, is worn on the cuffs of the special forces' grey-green collarless jacket, and stencilled on the left side of the helmet, which also bears a yellow fouled anchor. The 'San Marco' lapel patch was changed after September 1943; as was standard in the RSI forces, the national star was replaced with a wreathed *gladius* symbol, and the Lion of St Mark was also altered in detail – the book was closed, and the badge acquired at the bottom the Latin motto ITERUM RUDIT LEO ('The Lion Roars Again'). A lanyard in white/gold twist cord passes from his left shoulder into his pocket. On his left sleeve is the new metal badge of the Xª MAS Flotilla (**see detail 1a**); the skull-and-rose motif recalled a saying of Cdr Todaro of the 10th MAS surface assault craft, killed in December 1942, who had described death for the fatherland as something 'beautiful, perfumed'. He wears at the waist (obscured here) the canvas bag of the Beretta SMG, along with two triple pouches for its magazines. The jacket is characteristically worn with baggy paratroop trousers.

(2) *Sottotenente*, assault craft squadron; San Remo, summer 1944

The Navy's white summer cap has had the royal crown removed from the badge. The khaki cotton shirt is cut in Sahariana style. On the collar the national stars have been replaced with the RSI wreathed *gladius*, and on the dark blue uniform's shoulder boards the crown has been replaced with a fouled anchor, above the stars of rank. He, too, proudly sports the Xª MAS left sleeve shield.

(3) *Marò, Divisione Decima*; Piedmont, autumn 1944

This naval infantryman on anti-partisan duty wears the grey-green cotton version of the 'Sahariana' jacket, with paratroop trousers and boots. On the matching beret he wears the new naval badge introduced in July 1944 for members of the *Divisione Decima*, replacing a simple fouled anchor worn previously; the new cushion was supposed to be red, but grey-green was often seen. In midsummer 1944, after the RSI Army's 3rd 'San Marco' Div came back from training in Germany wearing the same red collar patches as the Xª MAS naval infantry, the latter replaced their red patches with these new blue ones, still showing the lion on a close-trimmed red backing above the wreathed shortsword. (The only exception was the 'Barbarigo' Bn, which kept the red patches to commemorate having been the first into the front line at Anzio.) Though it is not shown here, he might correctly wear a variant of the Xª MAS sleeve shield (**1a**) with the word 'DIVISIONE' in place of 'FLOTTIGLIA'. Again, the personal equipment is Mills-type khaki webbing, though here with only two large ammunition pouches.

1a

FLOTTIGLIA
MAS

Four 'marò' of the Xᵃ MAS posing in early 1944. Note that all wear 'Sahariana'- style jackets in grey-green cloth rather than the more common collarless jacket – see Plate F3. At right, a cloth version of the Xᵃ MAS sleeve shield is visible. (Molinari)

creation of another independent force unacceptable. By mid-November 1943 Ferrini was already trying to take control of the new naval infantry units by appointing a commander of his choice, and early in December he submitted to Mussolini a plan for the creation of a new naval infantry corps. On 16 December the new corps was officially formed, with a new command structure, and a plan to make it independent on 1 January 1944. However, on 9 January the 'Maestrale' Bn mutinied and arrested their new commander, which led in turn to Borghese's arrest by the RSI's police on 13 January. This 'game of chicken' reached a predictable conclusion: on 24 January Cdr Borghese was released and, on 13 February, Ferrini was replaced with Adm Giuseppe Sparzani. Four days later the latter was summoned to meet Dönitz, and learnt that in all but name Borghese's new infantry units would be under German rather than RSI Navy control. The outcome of this trial of strength was that Borghese achieved a unique freedom of action that enabled him to create, in effect, his own private army under overall Wehrmacht command.

Rome, early March 1944: the naval infantrymen of the 'Barbarigo' Bn parading in front of the German commander of the city, Gen Kurt Mältzer, on their way to the Anzio beachhead. This was the first unit of the RSI armed forces to be employed at the front against the Allies. (Molinari)

In January 1944 he formed another battalion, the 'Lupo', with an HQ and four companies (three rifle, one heavy weapons). By then the 'Barbarigo' (ex-'Maestrale') and the 'Lupo' at La Spezia totalled some 1,100 men, while Borghese had about another 1,200 – growing in February to 2,100 men – at La Spezia, plus 2,000 in other places. In February–March 1944 new units were formed or incorporated. The 'Fulmine' Bn had two companies mostly composed of Bersaglieri light infantry, and a third was added in July 1944 from volunteers repatriated from France. The 'Valanga' Guastatori Bn were mostly Alpini mountain infantrymen from an assault engineer unit formed on 29 September 1943 at Pavia with 200 men; it became part of Xᵃ MAS on 20 March 1944, with four companies (retitled 'Tarigo' in 1944, it later reverted to its old name). Others were the 'Freccia' communications battalion and the 'Castagnacci' training-and-replacement battalion. Many units were little more than names on paper or cadres, lacking weapons and equipment; for example, the 'Sagittario' Bn, between 100 and 400 strong depending upon the source, was formed in April 1944 by a group of Fascists from Trieste, and reorganized shortly thereafter. On 1 March a female auxiliary corps was even formed, the *Servizio Ausiliario Femminile*.

The Xᵃ MAS provided some 2,000 men for the creation of one of the four RSI Army divisions trained in Germany (3rd 'San Marco' Naval Inf Div), but the heterogeneous mixture of men still volunteering nevertheless allowed the Xᵃ MAS organization to increase in size. On 24 February 1944, when it was put under Borghese's supervision as Deputy Chief of Naval Staff, it included the 'San Marco' Div, the Xᵃ MAS units, and the coastal batteries under German command. On the suggestion of the German naval command in Italy, Borghese relinquished personal command of the original naval assault flotilla in May 1944.

Early operations

The Xᵃ MAS units were among the few RSI elements to see action in the front line against the Allies. Following the Anzio landing on 22 January 1944, one RSI paratroop and one Italian Waffen-SS battalion were sent to the area, along with the 800-strong 'Barbarigo' Battalion. This arrived on 4 March and was deployed on the Mussolini Canal south-east of the beachhead, under command of the German 715th Division. The Germans noted its overall lack of training and experience, but the 'Barbarigo' performed satisfactorily (mostly in patrol work), and showed a willingness to improve. In March–April two artillery batteries were also formed, with 105/28 and 105/32 guns; this core of the 'San Giorgio' Artillery Bn was to be followed by two other units, the 'Colleoni' and 'Da Giussano' battalions. On 19 May the 'Barbarigo' was down to a strength of 714; on 24 May it started the withdrawal that brought it first to Rome (where only 462 men arrived), then to northern Italy.

In March–April 1944 the German Army also took under operational control some other Xᵃ MAS units. On 16 April the Armeegruppe von Zangen, responsible for northern Italy, put the 'Lupo' Bn – 800 strong, but short of weapons and equipment – under command of the 'Hermann Göring' Division for training, and to fight the partisans around Pisa in Tuscany. The 'Sagittario' Bn was also employed in anti-partisan fighting, before being reorganized in the summer. In mid-May the 'NP' battalion also came under the control of Armeegruppe von Zangen, its sabotage/espionage company operating under command of a German intelligence unit, Maj Thun's Abwehrkommando 212.

The 'Divisione Decima'

Given the interest shown by the German Army, in April 1944 a proposal was made to form a combat group with four regiments (two naval infantry, one artillery and one special forces), for which eight Xª MAS battalions were to be made available: the 'Barbarigo' at Anzio; three others in training ('Lupo', 'NP' and 'Castagnacci'); and four others in process of formation ('Sagittario', 'Valanga', 'Fulmine' and 'Freccia'). There was also the cadre of the first of what would eventually be three artillery battalions; the first two batteries of this 'San Giorgio' Bn had been in action at Anzio with 105/28 and 105/32 howitzers. Three more infantry units were planned: the 'Sciré', 'Serenissima' and 'Vega' battalions.

At the end of April, Cdr Borghese suggested the formation of a naval infantry division for use against the partisans, to be assembled from all the available volunteers. Consequently, on 1 May 1944 the *Divisione Decima* (10th Division) was created – though mostly on paper – with the following organization as of early June 1944:

Headquarters (Cdr Luigi Carallo)
    'Freccia' Engineer Battalion (forming)
    'Castagnacci' Training & Replacement Bn (forming)
1° *Reggimento Fanteria di Marina* (LtCdr Bardelli)
    'Barbarigo' Bn (operational)
    'Lupo' Bn (operational)
    'NP' Bn (operational)
2° *Reggimento Fanteria di Marina* (forming)
    'Sagittario' Bn (forming)
    'Fulmine' Bn (forming)
    'Valanga' Bn (forming)
3° *Reggimento Artiglieria* 'Condottieri'
    1° *Gruppo* 'San Giorgio' (operational)
    2° *Gruppo* 'Da Giussano' (forming)
    3° *Gruppo* 'Colleoni' (forming)

Strength rose from 3,500 all ranks in early June 1944 to 4,776 at the end of that month. On 29 June, GenFM Kesselring, the German C-in-C Italy, put the Divisione Decima under command of the Higher SS & Police Commander Italy, SS-Gen Karl Wolff, for employment against the partisans. The battalions would never attain more than perhaps half-strength, but the announcement claimed that elite status counted for more than sheer numbers.

In July 1944 the battalions 'Barbarigo', 'Sagittario', 'Fulmine', 'Valanga', 'Freccia', part of the 'NP', the 'Colleoni' artillery and, from 10 August, the 'Lupo', were sent to the Canavese region of north-west Italy. They soon clashed with the partisans, and on 8 July the 1st Regt lost their Cdr Bardelli. In late July the *Raggruppamento Borghese* (Combat Group Borghese) was formed, taking under command the German I Bn/15. SS-Polizei Regt and elements of 208. Panzer Abteilung. With varying numbers of the Divisione Decima battalions under command, the group's strength fluctuated between 1,200 and 2,100 men plus 450 Germans. Over the period 31 July– 2 September 1944 it carried out a series of counter-insurgency operations in the Piedmont valleys, inflicting losses of 269 partisans killed, 2 wounded and 172 prisoners, at the cost of 30 killed (of which 6 were Germans), 95 wounded (45 Germans) and 23 missing. After the withdrawal of the

A heavily defended barracks of the Xᵃ MAS in northern Italy, 1943–44; in their security role these units had bases in many northern cities, including Milan, Turin, Genoa, La Spezia, Venice, Trieste and Fiume. In the foreground is a 20mm Breda anti-aircraft cannon, and to the right an 8mm Breda 37 machine gun. (Vitetti)

SS-Polizei battalion, in the period 5 September–5 October a new series of operations saw all the Divisione Decima battalions in action (the group's strength varying between 1,600 and 2,600). Partisan losses were 369 killed, 14 wounded and 190 captured, at the cost of 32 killed (2 Germans), 119 wounded (6 Germans) and 32 missing. Later in October 1944 the Divisione Decima was ordered to move to the Veneto region in north-eastern Italy.

Summer 1944: a group of Xᵃ MAS naval infantrymen of the *Divisione Decima* use an inflatable boat to cross a river in north-west Italy during one of the several anti-partisan sweeps in the wetlands of the Piedmont valleys. All are wearing shorts, along with some kind of loose smock in a pale shade. Although Xᵃ MAS units had been employed for this kind of duty since April, it was from summer 1944 that they became particularly associated with anti-partisan operations. (Vitetti)

A 'flotilla' swallows a navy

The new role of Borghese's X^a MAS, along with the crisis during summer 1944 that followed the Allied advance to the Gothic Line and the general uprising of Italian partisans, led to a clash between the RSI authorities and the Kriegsmarine high command in Italy. Given the diminished role of the Italian naval assault forces relative to their own, and openly casting doubt on the loyalty of many naval personnel, the Germans demanded that the RSI provide them with manpower for employment in anti-aircraft and smoke units. On 9 August 1944 a reorganization of the Navy began under Borghese's leadership. All naval units – which mostly consisted of services and logistical elements – were put under a single command; part of the personnel were transferred to anti-partisan duties, and most commands and units were formally incorporated into the X^a MAS.

This allowed the formation of new infantry units: to the already planned 'Sciré', 'Serenissima' and 'Vega' were now added new 'Risoluti', 'San Giusto' and 'Pegaso' battalions, plus an AA battalion, four detachments, and five independent companies. By 1 November 1944 the X^a MAS organization had reached a total strength of 7,615 men (8,395 by 1 March 1945), out of the RSI Navy's overall manpower of 13,663. By 1945, indeed, the Navy had been almost entirely absorbed into the X^a MAS. The actual field strength of the Divisione Decima was not affected, however; this increased only slightly, from 3,400 to 3,600, between September 1944 and March 1945. On 26 March 1945, Cdr Borghese was appointed Chief of the Naval Staff.

Operations, December 1944–April 1945

While the bulk of the Divisione Decima regrouped for a transfer eastwards, the 'Lupo' Bn was attached early in December 1944 to the 16. SS-Panzergrenadier Div 'Reichsführer-SS' to fight in the Apennine Mountains,

X^a MAS FLOTILLA; ITALY, 1944–45

(1) *Guardiamarina*, MAS squadron; San Remo, summer 1944

This torpedo motorboat commander wears the same cap badge and shoulder boards as Plate F2, but with a long-sleeved 'Sahariana' and trousers. The collar patches are those adopted by the surviving maritime assault units of the flotilla: white, with a gold fouled anchor above a silver wreathed *gladius*. His most junior commissioned rank but several awards suggest that he is a promoted former petty officer with long experience. On his left breast is an Assault Craft Service Badge, one of a series introduced in May 1944 in three classes. Below this are ribbons for the Bronze War Medal of Honour, War Merit Cross, and War Service Badge, and that of the German Iron Cross 2nd Class is worn from his buttonhole.

(2) *Capitano di fregata* Junio Valerio Borghese, 1944

Commander Borghese, simultaneously commanding the X^a MAS organization and holding the appointment of Deputy Chief of Naval Staff (Operations), wears the naval beret with the new RSI cap badge surmounted by an eagle, and the two 'boxed' stars of his rank. His Army-style grey-green service uniform is worn with a matching shirt and necktie. In addition to his grey-green shoulder boards of rank, the same collar patches as G1, and the flotilla sleeve shield, he displays numerous awards. On his right pocket is the X^a MAS Honour

Badge (**see detail 2a**), awarded to personnel who rallied immediately after the September 1943 surrender. Above his left pocket are three awards: the new War Merit Promotion Badge, and the old service badges for both assault-craft and submarine personnel. Below these are the ribbons for the Gold and Silver War Medals of Honour, followed by (although it should precede them) the Military Order of Savoy. His German Iron Cross 1st Class is pinned to his left pocket, and the 2nd Class ribbon is sewn from his buttonhole. Borghese was often photographed carrying a 9mm Walther P38 pistol in a simple strapping skeleton-holster on a shoulder sling.

(3) *Marò*, 'Lupo' Battalion; Senio river, January 1945

This naval infantryman, awaiting the British offensive on the eastern half of the Gothic Line defences, wears a helmet crudely camouflaged with paint; the red 'X' of the flotilla is just visible on the left side. Rollneck or – as here – zipped sweaters were commonly worn with the grey-green special forces uniform. This 1944 smock made from Italian camouflage material, with Sahariana-style pocket flaps extended into a shoulder cape, was widely used by X^a MAS personnel, often with trousers of the same pattern; note the silver RSI badges on its wide collar. He carries magazines for his Beretta M38A SMG in a set of German MP40 pouches, and has been issued German stick grenades and a *Panzerfaust* anti-tank rocket.

Men of the 5th (Heavy Weapons) Co of the 'NP' Bn in the square of a Venetian town in February 1945; note the 8mm Breda 37 MGs, with their tripods carried by the men on the right. All are wearing the blue lapel patches adopted by Xª MAS units in summer 1944, to set them apart from the German-trained 3rd Naval Inf Div 'San Marco' of the *Esercito Nazionale Repubblicano*. Most also display the Xª MAS shield, and parachute or 'NP' qualification badges either on the sleeve or the chest. (Vitetti)

while in the same month the 'Valanga' and 'Fulmine' battalions operated against partisans in the Venice area. By mid-December the bulk of the division (the 'Sagittario', 'Fulmine' and 'Barbarigo' Bns, elements from the 'NP' and 'Freccia', and the 'San Giorgio' and 'Da Giussano' artillery units) were deployed on the German-controlled eastern border with Slovenia to fight the Yugoslav partisans; meanwhile the 'Valanga', part of the 'Freccia' and the artillery 'Colleoni' battalion were left in the Venice area. The operations along the eastern border did not get off to an auspicious start; during mopping-up operations of 19–31 December the 'Decima's' Cdr Carallo was killed, to be replaced with Gen Giuseppe Corrado. In January 1945 two combat groups were formed ('Fulmine' and 'Sagittario' in one, 'Barbarigo', 'Valanga' and 'NP' in the other), and deployed along the Natisone and Isonzo valleys. Just before leaving for the front, on 19 January the 'Fulmine' was attacked by Yugoslav partisans in its isolated post at Selva di Tarnova; surrounded for two days before reinforcements arrived, the battalion was left with 131 men out of its original, and already feeble strength of 214.

Men of the 3rd Co, 'Lupo' Bn on the Senio river in January 1945. Apart from the man on the left, who has a cape-shouldered camouflage smock, they all wear the collarless grey-green jacket; the man on the far right displays full Xᵃ MAS insignia. The central figure (with two German stick grenades in his belt) is *Marò* Alberto Bellagamba, who on New Year's Eve destroyed the Sherman tank visible on the right with a German *Panzerfaust*. (Molinari)

In early February the units of the division were regrouped again in the Vicenza area, fighting against partisans while a badly needed reorganization took place in preparation for the deployment of one combat group to the front line. In the face of heavy losses, four of the newly created battalions were disbanded and their personnel dispersed as replacements, along with men taken from the naval services and territorial organization. As of 15 March 1945, the new organization was as follows:

Officers of the 'Lupo' Bn photographed in March 1945 during a pause behind the lines. The lieutenant in the foreground wears the type of cape-shouldered smock shown in Plate G3. On a pale yellow area of the collar can be seen the Lion of St Mark badge on a closely trimmed red backing, above the wreathed shortsword, and on his left chest below this he has attached his naval cuff ranking. He wears a shirt and necktie, while the centre officer has chosen the commonly seen zipped woollen pullover. (Molinari)

I *Gruppo Combattimento 'Sciré'* (LtCdr Antonio De Giacomo)
  'Lupo' Bn (until February 1945)
  'Barbarigo' Bn
  'NP' Bn
  'Colleoni' Artillery Bn
  one company, 'Freccia' Engineer Bn
II *Gruppo Combattimento 'Castagnacci'* (LtCdr Corrado de Martino)
  'Sagittario' Bn
  'Fulmine' Bn
  'Valanga' Bn
  'San Giorgio' Arty Bn
  'Da Giussano' Arty Bn
  'Castagnacci' Replacement Bn
  two cos, 'Freccia' Engr Bn

The 'Lupo' Bn, in action since December 1944, was sent north of the River Po in February 1945. In March the German Tenth Army deployed the I Combat Group (totalling some 1,400 men) on the Senio river in the eastern part of the front, facing V Corps of the British Eighth Army. The other 2,200-odd men of the Divisione Decima remained in the Vicenza area. I Combat Group faced the last Allied offensive in April 1945, all of them surrendering later that same month. (It is worth noting that selected personnel from the X^a MAS formed a 'stay-behind' organization supplied with money and hidden weapons caches, which was quickly dismantled after the end of the war. Supposedly, some of its members worked for Allied intelligence agencies thereafter.)

Men of the *I Gruppo Combattimento* of the *Divisione Decima* on the Senio river front in spring 1945; the first two each carry a *Panzerfaust*. This area, close to the Adriatic coast, is characterized by streams and rivers with steep banks – a hindrance for the advancing Allies. (Vitetti)

'FOLGORE' PARACHUTE REGIMENT, 1943–45

In September 1943 numbers of Army and Air Force paratroopers chose to join the Germans to continue the fight. They included Army personnel from XII Bn/184th Regt and III Bn/185th Regt of the 'Nembo' Div, plus elements from the then-forming 'Ciclone' Div and the X Arditi, and from the Air Force ADRA Battalion. Totalling about 350 men, they were assembled into a *Raggruppamento Volontari Paracadutisti* under command of the German 2. Fallschirmjäger Div, stationed along the Tyrrhenian coast west of Rome. A continuing flow of volunteers brought strength up to 760 in November 1943; and on 25 December the commander of German airborne forces, Gen Kurt Student, ordered the formation around this nucleus of an Italian paratroop regiment, with a planned strength of 2,200 in four battalions, within the then-forming 4. Fallschirmjäger Division. Meanwhile, on 1 December, a *Scuola Paracadutisti della RSI* was set up at Tradate in northern Italy by the RSI's Air Force (*Aeronautica Nazionale Repubblicana*, ANR). Formation of the planned regiment began, from personnel sent to the Spoleto area north of Rome; 150 selected men were sent to the German parachute school at Freiburg, and another group on a specialization course held near Avignon in France.

Members of the 'Folgore' Parachute Regt in summer 1944, wearing Italian uniforms and camouflage jump-smocks but with some German equipment, including a map case and an MP40 submachine gun. Some heavier weapons such as the MG42 were provided, but not in large numbers. The one-eyed first lieutenant at right displays the old-style parachute sleeve badge, and the cuff title '8-9-43 PER L'ONORE D'ITALIA'. This was awarded to those who rallied to the Fascist cause immediately upon the Italian surrender of 8 September 1943; those who joined the regiment subsequently received the cuff title without the date numerals. (Vitetti)

A *sergente maggiore* (one thick above two thin gold sleeve chevrons) of the 'Folgore' Regt in late 1944. He wears the regiment's blue lapel patches with a winged dagger above the RSI's wreathed shortsword. On his left breast is the 1942 Air Force parachutist's gold 'wings' brevet, and he wears the later qualification badge (illustrated as Plate H2a) above his left sleeve chevrons. Note the cuff title 'PER L'ONORE D'ITALIA' (see Plate H2). He also has the ribbon of the German Iron Cross 2nd Class in his buttonhole, and as a keepsake he wears on his pocket the *Edelweiss* cap badge of a German mountain trooper – no doubt acquired when the regiment was attached to 5. Gebirgs Division. (Molinari)

The Tradate parachute school included a *Raggruppamento Arditi Paracadutisti ANR* under command of LtCol Edvino Dalmas; in fact this was simply an HQ, which in January 1944 started to form a battalion named 'Azzurro' for the new *Arditi Distruttori Aeronautica Repubblicana* (APAR), stemming directly from the pre-surrender ADRA. By March 1944 the *Raggruppamento* and the battalion would together total some 900 all ranks.

The actual formation of paratroop units was hampered by the difficulties of gathering and training all the available men from different units and backgrounds. (In February 1944, some 20 per cent of the Italian personnel being transferred to Spoleto for the new regiment went 'absent without leave', although in many cases these men would join German units to fight at the front.)

The first battalion of the new 'Folgore' Regt was only created after the Allied landings at Anzio in January 1944. This *Battaglione Paracadutisti 'Nembo'*, formed in late January, was only 433 strong, with two companies. With other units of the German 4. FJ Div it was sent to Anzio under command of Capt Corradino Alvino, arriving on 10 February to be deployed in the north-west sector. Although not involved in the major infantry fighting the unit suffered seriously from a lack of proper training. Early in March, after a few attacks against British positions, the battalion practically broke down, with many men going absent and others suffering from combat shock. In late March–early April 1944 Italian paratroopers took part in anti-partisan operations in the rear areas around the Anzio beachhead, but in April the 'Nembo' Bn was down to a single company named 'Nettunia-Nembo' (Nettunia was the collective Italian name for Anzio and Nettuno), and on 19 May only 152 out of the original 433 men were left.

In late April 1944 the 'Folgore' Regt had finally been formed from personnel gathered at Spoleto during March–April and volunteers brought in by a new recruitment drive. On 1 May the Italian paratroopers formally became part of the Air Force, following the German practice. On the 19th of that month the 'Azzurro' Bn was transferred into the new *Reggimento Paracadutisti 'Folgore'*. Commanded by LtCol Dalmas, on 27 May the regiment had a total strength of 1,200 Italians and 130 Germans (plus the men of the 'Nettunia-Nembo' Co), organized as follows:

I Battaglione *'Folgore'* (Maj Rizzati), 1st–4th Companies
II Battaglione *'Nembo'* (Capt Recchia), 5th–8th Cos
III Battaglione *'Azzurro'* (Capt Bussoli), 9th–12th Cos

* * *

After the Allied breakout from the Cassino line and the Anzio beachhead, early in June most of the 'Folgore' Regt was deployed to the south of Rome to act as a rearguard: II Bn, with three companies from I Bn and three from III Battalion. The Italian paratroopers distinguished themselves in combat against superior Allied forces, earning the approval of the German Fourteenth Army, and on 10 June the 'Folgore' was mentioned in German despatches;

but their losses were severe, including Maj Rizzati and many German officers and NCOs. Subsequently many companies were disbanded when their retreat was cut off by the River Tiber; a similar fate saw the end of the 'Nettunia-Nembo' Co from Anzio, which reached Rome 120 strong but was soon down to ten men.

What was left of the 'Folgore' Regt was withdrawn from the line and sent north to Tradate for rebuilding. General Student repeatedly asked permission to form another Italian paratroop regiment, but this was twice refused by GenFM Kesselring. In late June 1944 there were 647 paratroopers at Tradate, and in July new recruits were used to rebuild the regiment with the former structure. On 1 November 1944 the title was changed to *1° Reggimento Arditi Paracadutisti 'Folgore'*, still under command of LtCol Dalmas, with I Bn 'Folgore' led by Capt Sala, II Bn 'Nembo' (Capt Alvino) and III Bn 'Azzurro' (Capt Bussoli). Following his promotion in January 1945, Maj Sala took over the regimental command.

While still re-forming in July 1944 the regiment was thrown into action against partisans in the Turin area, and then in north-west Italy until October. Early that month the regiment was regrouped again at Turin under command of German LXXV Corps, attached first to the 157. Inf Div and then to the 5. Gebirgs Division. The regiment was deployed in the north-western Alps, opposite Free French forces in the areas of the Moncenisio and Piccolo San Bernardo mountains. Facing both the Allies on the western side of the Alps and the partisan threat from their rear, the paratroopers were eventually more active against the latter. From 5 November 1944 to 15 February 1945 they inflicted partisan losses of 76 killed, 36 wounded and 182 prisoners, for a cost of 11 killed, 36 wounded and 5 missing.

The Assault Parachute Regiment 'Folgore' finally surrendered to US forces late in April 1945 in the Valle d'Aosta.

Paratroopers of the 'Folgore' Regt in the western Alps, 1944–45. The left man has the German reversible camouflage/white padded winter jacket and matching trousers, and his comrades the German reversible field-grey/white mountain anorak with three chest pockets (see Plate H3). The belts are German, but with the new buckle of the Italian paratroopers. All carry holstered Beretta M34 pistols. (Vitetti)

CONCLUSIONS

The striking contrast between the achievements of *10ᵃ Flottiglia MAS* in naval special warfare in 1940–42, and the sparse successes of the 'San Marco' Naval Infantry and of the Air Force airborne special units, makes some kind of conclusion necessary.

The most obvious advantage enjoyed by the former over the latter was that the 10th MAS was a 'bottom-upwards' concept, which could trace the development – by genuinely visionary officers – of its doctrine, equipment and training back to 1935. The naval landing battalions, by contrast, were born of a 'top-downwards' initiative – and a shockingly half-hearted one, at that – and were never given the necessary equipment and training to allow them to become true specialists. In the case of 10th MAS, special capabilities and equipment were developed first, before suitable objectives were assigned; by contrast, the unfortunate Air Force paratroop units were rushed into existence in a few months to meet a belatedly identified tactical need.

 'FOLGORE' PARACHUTE REGIMENT; ITALY, 1944–45

(1) *Paracadutista*, 'Nembo' Battalion; Anzio, early 1944
Since the battalion was formed within the German 4. Fallschirmjäger Division, it was not unusual for members of the companies fighting at Anzio to wear – as here – the German 'splinter-pattern' jump-smock rather than the Italian equivalent. The rest of the uniform and equipment was largely Italian, with widespread use of the 'Samurai' ammo vests.

(2) *Sottotenente*; Rome front, June 1944
The basic uniform worn by the Air Force paratroopers changed little after the surrender: a beret, collarless jacket and baggy trousers in Air Force blue-grey. Sweaters were often worn instead of shirts, and many items of German equipment were issued – like the map case carried by this second lieutenant. The old beret badge has the crown removed, and is worn with the single star of this rank. The lapel patches now have a gold sword set on a silver grenade with red flames, and gold wings, all above the usual silver

wreath and *gladius*. On the left upper sleeve is the new RSI parachute qualification badge (**see detail 2a**), with a *gladius* and flaming grenade set on the parachute between laurel and oak branches. As a graduate of the Freiburg jump school, he also wears the German qualification badge on his left pocket. Note, above his left cuff ranking, a regimental cuff title in black edged with the national colours (red, white, green, reading inwards) and bearing 'PER L'ONORE D'ITALIA' in orange-red lettering. His belt has the new paratrooper's silver buckle, bearing a large eagle superimposed over a parachute.

(3) *Paracadutista*; Western Alps, February 1945
When deployed in the Alps under the German 5th Mountain Division the regiment were extensively re-equipped. With his Italian beret and trousers this paratrooper wears a German 1942 hooded, reversible mountain anorak with three chest pockets (and provision for a crotch-strap), and German mountain boots. Ammunition for the now almost ubiquitous Beretta SMG is carried in a German MP40 triple magazine pouch, and this man also has a Beretta M34 pistol.

Spring 1942: men of the 'San Marco' Regt take part in a landing exercise in preparation for the planned seaborne assault against Malta. The landing vessels, apparently some sort of commandeered fishing boats, are clearly completely inadequate for the purpose. This kind of neglect robbed the sea-landing troops of any chance of success in a resisted beach landing. (AUSSM)

There is no doubt that the achievements of the 10th MAS were remarkable, and not only by Italian standards. Its unique skills and experience were widely acknowledged, amongst others by the German Kriegsmarine, which took it as a model for its own special assault units. Nevertheless, one should not exaggerate the effects of these achievements on the course of the naval war in the Mediterranean, and one must acknowledge that they decreased noticeably after the successful raid on Alexandria harbour in December 1941. That moment marked the peak of the flotilla's efforts, and it should have offered the best opportunity to mount a subsequent Axis assault on Malta, to seize once and for all control of the central Mediterranean and of the supply routes to Libya.

This was the very purpose for which both the Navy landing units and the Air Force special forces were created. There were many reasons why the planned assault never took place, not the least of them being Rommel's ultimately fatal decision to invade Egypt and advance on Alexandria in spring/summer 1942. The cancellation of the operation led to the useless and wasteful dissipation of the specialist units as conventional infantry in Tunisia, Corsica and southern France.

Commander Borghese with Gen Hildebrandt, commanding general of the German 715. Infanterie Division, to which Xª MAS troops were attached. Borghese wears the standard grey-green officer's greatcoat, with the white lapel patches of the post-surrender naval assault unit. Note his habitual Walther P38 pistol. (Vitetti)

No meaningful comparison can be made between the performance of the 10th MAS in 1940–42 and that of the Xª MAS and paratroop units in 1943–45, although the latter formed the nearest to an elite that the RSI forces could boast. Like the Navy landing battalions and Air Force special forces before them, their lack of adequate training and preparation made their relatively poor performance – particularly at Anzio – inevitable. These factors, along with inadequate command and leadership, are the main reasons behind the often deprecated lack of combat effectiveness amongst the wartime Italian armed forces in general. This betrayal of the courage and willingness of the junior ranks is simply unusually striking in the case of the potentially elite units.

SELECT BIBLIOGRAPHY

Arena, Nino, *I paracadutisti italiani 1937–45* (Milan, 1989)

Bagnasco, Erminio, *Le navi d'Italia. Mas e mezzi d'assalto di superficie italiani* (Rome, 1996)

Bagnasco, Erminio, & Mario Spertini, *I mezzi d'assalto della X Flottiglia Mas (1940–45)* (Parma, 2005)

Battistelli, Pier Paolo & Andrea Molinari, *Le forze armate della RSI* (Milan, 2007)

Bertucci, Aldo, *Guerra segreta dietro le linee* (Milan, 1995)

Bonvicini, Guido, *Decima marinai! Decima Comandante!* (Milan, 1988)

Borghese, Junio Valerio, *Decima Flottiglia MAS. Dalle origini all'armistizio* (Milan, 1950)

De Risio, Carlo, *La Marina Italiana nella II Guerra Mondiale. I mezzi d'assalto* (Rome, 2001)

Del Giudice, Elio & Vittorio, *La marina militare italiana. Uniformi, fregi e distintivi dal 1861 a oggi* (Parma, 1997)

Fulvi, L., Manzari G., Marcon T. & Miozzi O., *Le fanterie di marina italiane* (Rome, 1997)

Gabriele, Mariano, *La Marina Italiana nella II Guerra Mondiale. Operazione C3* (Rome, 1990)

Galuppini, Gino, *Le uniformi della marina militare* (Rome, 1999)

Giorgerini, Giorgio, *Attacco dal mare* (Milan, 2007)

Greene, Jack & Alessandro Massignani, *The Black Prince and the Sea Devils* (Cambridge, MA, 2004)

Kemp, Paul, *Midget Submarines of the Second World War* (London, 1999)

Longo, Luigi Emilio, *I "reparti speciali" italiani nella seconda guerra mondiale* (Milan, 1991)

Lundari, Giuseppe, *I paracadutisti italiani 1937–45* (Milan, 1989)

Lupinacci, Pier Francesco, *La Marina Italiana nella II Guerra Mondiale. Attività in Mar Nero e Lago Ladoga* (Rome, 2003)

Nesi, Sergio, *Decima flottiglia nostra* (Milan, 1986)

Paterson, Lawrence, *Weapons of Desperation. German Frogmen and Midget Submarines of the Second World War* (London, 2006)

Turrini A., Miozzi O. & Moreno M., *Le navi d'Italia. Sommergibili e mezzi d'assalto subacquei italiani* (Rome, 2010)

Ufficio Storico Marina Militare, *La Marina nella Guerra di Liberazione e nella Resistenza. Convegno di Studi di Venezia* (Rome, 1996)

Viotti, Andrea, *Aeronautica Italiana. Uniformi e distintivi nella II Guerra Mondiale* (Rome, 1989)

Zarotti, Andrea, *I Nuotatori Paracadutisti* (Milan, no date)

INDEX

Note: locators in **bold** refer to plates and illustrations.